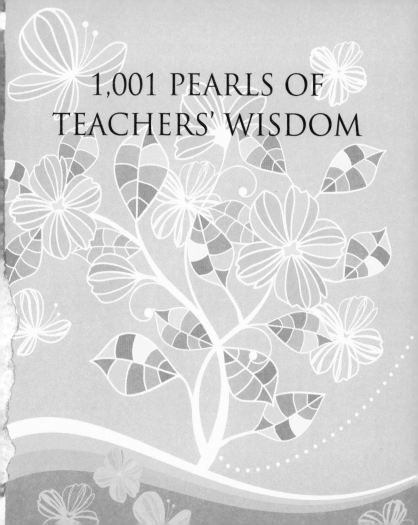

1,001 PEARLS OF
TEACHERS' WISDOM

1,001 PEARLS OF TEACHERS' WISDOM

Quotations on Life and Learning

EDITED BY ERIN GRUWELL
FOREWORD BY FRANK MCCOURT

Skyhorse Publishing

Skyhorse Publishing books may be purchased in bulk at special discounts for sales promotion, corporate gifts, fund-raising, or educational purposes. Special editions can also be created to specifications. For details, contact the Special Sales Department, Skyhorse Publishing, 307 West 36th Street, 11th Floor, New York, NY 10018 or info@skyhorsepublishing.com.

Skyhorse® and Skyhorse Publishing® are registered trademarks of Skyhorse Publishing, Inc.®, a Delaware corporation.

www.skyhorsepublishing.com

10 9 8 7 6 5 4 3 2 1

Library of Congress Cataloging-in-Publication Data is available on file.

Print ISBN: 978-1-5107-0643-9
ebook ISBN: 978-1-5107-1090-0

Printed in China

Table of Contents

Foreword
Frank McCourt

Teaching, as I've written elsewhere, is the downstairs maid of the professions. Teachers are not consulted when big decisions are being made about education. The decisions are made by politicians—for they know what is good for us. Frequently, there are panel discussions on education on television. There are politicians, people from think tanks, professors of education, bureaucrats. No teachers.

This is when I want to reach for a gun—but I don't, of course. I have to resort to my mouth. I try to be patient while I explain to the rich man that the teacher starting salary in this country is barely above poverty level. He looks doubtful when I ask him if he could support a wife and, at least, one child on a salary way under forty thousand dollars a year.

I'm not too agile when discussing the status of teachers in this country. I know they are underpaid. I know there is little respect for them despite the wonderful things said about them in this terrific book.

When I talked with the rich man, I hadn't yet read *1,001 Pearls of Teachers' Wisdom*—if "read" is the right word for what you do with this book. You're not going to sit in your easy chair and actually read it. It's a book for dipping into, a bowl of peanuts (bet you can't read just one!), a literary gazpacho. Maybe, when this book is published, I'll send the rich man a copy. He will find a few negative comments about teachers, but they're more than balanced by the high praise of teachers by perceptive men and women down the ages.

Here is God's plenty. Between the opening entry, "Teaching is truth mediated by personality," to the closing "Whatever you are, be a good one," there is a word hoard the likes of which you rarely see between the covers of a book.

I don't know what Phyllis Brooks (1915–1995) means by that opening statement, nor do I know whom she was. The book says she was an actress, and I wonder how she achieved pride of place. It just goes to show that everyone has something to say about teachers and teaching.

This last entry about being a "good one" is attributed to Abraham Lincoln, but it doesn't sound like him. Maybe he was depressed at the time. Maybe the war was going against him. Maybe the remark was made to someone aching for a platitude.

I would direct the rich man to fields of gold where there are nuggets of wisdom. Tolerate me from a moment while I offer choice morsels:

"Everyone who is incapable of learning has taken to teaching." Oscar Wilde (1854–1900)

I am sorry to inform you that Oscar, like myself, was an Irishman, of the Island of Saints and Scholars, and that smartass remark goes hand in hand with another smartass remark by George Bernard Shaw: "Those who can, do; those who can't, teach."

Oscar and George were brilliant men with encyclopedic minds, but about teaching they knew *bupkus*. (That's a Yiddish word for bugger all.)

But don't worry: a few pages later, Shaw redeems himself. He says, "To me the sole hope of human salvation lies in teaching." Right on, Mr. Shaw, and would you pass the word to Oscar, wherever you are, the two of you exhausting the angels with your witty discourse, the two of you knowing full well you were teachers yourselves.

Jump ahead a few years and you find Lee Iacocca urging everyone to "Apply yourself. Get all the education you can, but then, by God, do something. Don't just stand there, make it happen."

A generation later comes this bullet of common sense from T. J. O'Rourke: "Anyway, no drug, not even alcohol, causes the fundamental ills of society. If we're looking for the source of our troubles, we shouldn't test people for drugs, we should test them for stupidity, ignorance, greed, and love of power."

Back to the world of teaching. Here is Ann Richards (1933–2006), former governor of Texas: "Teaching was the hardest work I had ever done, and it remains the hardest work I have done to date."

Here is one I love from Ignacio Estrada: "If a child can't learn the way we teach, maybe we should teach the way they learn." I don't know who Ignacio Estrada is, but wherever he is I want to blow kisses and pin medals to his wise chest, for his comment sums it up for me.

If only the politicians and the rich would pay attention to Ignacio and teachers would teach the way he suggests. If only the politicians would get off that broken nag called No Child Left Behind and stop testing our children till they're numb and senseless and incapable of even thinking.

Listen to Robert Hutchins (1899–1977): "It must be remembered that the purpose of education is not to fill the minds of students with facts . . . it is to teach them to think, if that is possible, and always to think of themselves."

Mr. Hutchins, Mr. Hutchins, stay where you are. You'd be appalled at what is happening in our schools. We are not encouraging thinking. We are killing young minds. We are engaged in some strange activity called "setting standards." We are sucking the dream out of the classroom. Our teachers are on edge, looking over their shoulders, worried their students won't score high on those insane tests.

The rich man sitting next to me at the party assures me that the salaries of New York teachers are more than adequate. He tells me also how lucky teachers are that they get all that time off. They get all the holidays, he tells me, and they get those long summers. Also, they don't work a full day like other "professionals."

Teachers? When did you last see a teacher on any kind of talk show?

1,001 Pearls of Teachers' Wisdom will, maybe, call attention to the "real" world of teaching. Take your time with it. Keep it by your bed. It wouldn't hurt to read a few lines to your children at bedtime. They might grow and become teachers.

And wouldn't that rock the country!

Frank McCourt

Introduction
Erin Gruwell

As educators, we share one common goal—to see the growth and progress of our students. But one thing is for sure—there is no greater feeling than to see a student "get it." You know what that's like. It's when things "click" in a young mind. It's when the proverbial light bulb goes on. It's when you see eyes light up in revelry. It's when you see a student accomplish what he or she once thought was impossible. There's nothing better. It is for this reason that we show up to work each day.

One of the greatest lessons I learned from the Freedom Writers was that in order to be a good teacher, I had to be an even better student. The Freedom Writers had what I like to call a "PhD of the Streets," and I quickly found I had 150 teachers who would help me "get it" on a daily basis! My students became savvy teachers and amazed me each and every day with their personal insight and knowledge.

My students taught me a simple lesson: to teach to a student, and not to a test. They taught me to be open to new theories, practices, and modes of thinking, because each student learns in a different way. Not all students pick up the same lessons at the same speed, learn through the same modalities, or grasp ideas by the same means and methods. What works for one may not work for another. Learning is a process.

To help me in the learning process, I found the usage of quotations in my classroom an extremely powerful tool. Not only were they lessons on diversity of opinion, but they also taught about the world as a whole. Quotations became a vehicle that made it easy to transport a wealth of knowledge to the Freedom Writers. For example, when we met the Holocaust survivor Renee Firestone, she poignantly told my students, "Evil prevails when good people do nothing." We posted Renee's quotation on the chalkboard, and it became a rallying cry for my students. They decided that they would no longer stand idly by and watch injustice unfurl. In a similar vein, they continued to find quotations that encouraged them to become social activists, such as Gandhi's "Be the change you want to see in the world." With the inspiration of such powerful quotations, they were, and continue to be, the most powerful young activists I have ever known.

People interpret quotations differently, but we know that one jewel or that one glimmer of hope when we see it.

It stares us straight in the face. Becoming better human beings on all levels was my students' goal, and opening their eyes to leading a more positive way of life was mine. So using powerful quotations from the young diarist Anne Frank, who wrote, "In spite of everything, I truly believe that people are good at heart," became another teachable moment.

My students, like so many others, needed a few words of encouragement and relevance when times got rough to keep them focused on what truly mattered—the success and personal growth of their own lives. Soon my students were incorporating quotations into like "What doesn't kill me will make me stronger" or "If we don't learn from history, we are doomed to repeat it" into their daily lives. Suddenly, the usage of quotations allowed them to articulate their dreams of rising above their circumstances.

Since their graduation from Woodrow Wilson High School in 1998, the Freedom Writers have gone on to bigger and better things. They have set—and stuck to—even loftier goals than before. They have compiled their journal entries to craft a *New York Times* #1 bestselling book, *The Freedom Writers Diary* (1999); won numerous awards for outstanding leadership; and been covered in countless media stories. Ironically, now students and teachers use powerful quotations from their book for inspiration, such as our class motto, "When diverse worlds come together, beauty is inevitable!"

Today, the Freedom Writers are teachers, journalists, filmmakers, and music industry professionals. A few even help run the Freedom Writers Foundation, the nonprofit organization we started to promote acceptance and innovative teaching methods in classrooms across the world. None of this would have been possible without the words of authors, poets, and activists, some of whom are quoted in this book.

In the pages of *The Gigantic Book of Teachers' Wisdom*, you will find pearls of wisdom that encourage creative thinking. The book is a compilation of thought-provoking, inspiring quotations that you will identify with and hopefully pass along to your students through the course of their academic careers. Since the quotations are insightful and poignant, I suggest you read them aloud in class, write them on the board, or simply hold onto the gems of wisdom that mean the most to you.

My hope is that as you read through *The Gigantic Book of Teachers' Wisdom*, you are continually inspired by the words within its pages, in the same way that the Freedom Writers have inspired me. This book was created for those who "fight the good fight" every day and who revel in seeing their students mature, little by little, into hopeful young adults.

Erin Gruwell

THE TEACHER

Teaching is not a lost art, but the regard for it is a lost tradition.
—Jacques Barzun

The difficulty is to try and teach the multitude that something can be true and untrue at the same time.
—Arthur Schopenhauer

Teaching is truth mediated by personality.
—Phyllis Brooks

Teaching is the achievement of shared meaning.
—D.B. Gowin

Teaching is the perpetual end and office of all things. Teaching, instruction is the main design that shines through the sky and earth.
—RALPH WALDO EMERSON

The whole art of teaching is only the art of awakening the natural curiosity of young minds for the purpose of satisfying it afterwards; and curiosity itself can be vivid and wholesome only in proportion as the mind is contented and happy.
—ANATOLE FRANCE

The most important part of teaching is to teach what it is to know.
—SIMONE WEIL

TEACHING: The earth doesn't move every time, but when it does, what a RUSH!
—Cameron Beatty

Teaching is the greatest act of optimism.
—Colleen Wilcox

If the student fails to learn, the teacher fails to teach.
—Anonymous

If kids come to educators and teachers from strong, healthy, functioning families, it makes our job easier. If they do not come to us from strong, healthy, functioning families, it makes our job more important.
—Barbara Colorose

Teaching is the only major occupation of man for which we have not yet developed tools that make an average person capable of competence and performance. In teaching we rely on the "naturals," the ones who somehow know how to teach.
—Peter Drucker

The art of teaching is the art of assisting discovery.
—Mark Van Doren

Teachers are expected to reach unattainable goals with inadequate tools. The miracle is that at times they accomplish this impossible task.
—Dr. Haim Ginott

I cannot teach anybody anything. I can only make them think.

—SOCRATES

I do not teach. I relate.

—MONTAIGNE

We all need someone who inspires us to do better than we know how.

—ANONYMOUS

In teaching you cannot see the fruit of a day's work. It is invisible and remains so, maybe for twenty years.

—JACQUES BARZUN

It must be remembered that the purpose of education is not to fill the minds of students with facts . . . it is to teach them to think, if that is possible, and always to think for themselves.
—ROBERT HUTCHINS

The secret of teaching is to appear to have known all your life what you learned this afternoon.
—ANONYMOUS

Teaching was the hardest work I had ever done, and it remains the hardest work I have done to date.
—ANN RICHARDS

The work of a teacher—exhausting, complex, idiosyncratic, never twice the same—is at its heart, an intellectual and ethical enterprise. Teaching is the vocation of vocations . . .
—WILLIAM AYRES

Good teaching is one-fourth preparation and three-fourths theater.
—GAIL GODWIN

The important thing is not so much that every child should be taught, as that every child should be given the wish to learn.
—JOHN LUBBOCK

You cannot teach a man anything; you can only help him find it within himself.
—GALILEO GALILEI

To teach is to learn twice.
—JOSEPH JOUBERT

In teaching, it is the method and not the content that is the message . . . the drawing out, not the pumping in.
—ASHLEY MONTAGUE

The object of teaching a child is to enable him to get along without his teacher.
—ELBERT HUBBARD

To me the sole hope of human salvation lies in teaching.
—George Bernard Shaw

When teaching, light a fire, don't fill a bucket.
—Dan Snow

Teaching is the profession that teaches all the other professions.
—Anonymous

When you teach your son, you teach your son's son.
—Talmud Rabbinical writings

Only a teacher? Thank God I have a calling to the greatest profession of all!
—Ivan Welton Fitzwater

Teachers can change lives with just the right mix of chalk and challenges.
—Joyce A. Myers, from her book How Much Is Enough? (1957)

The temple that teachers built will last while ages roll, for that beautiful unseen temple is the child's eternal soul.
—St. Ambrose, Catholic bishop of Milan

Good teaching must be slow enough so that it is not confusing, and fast enough so that it is not boring.
—Sidney J. Harris

Effective teaching may be the hardest job there is.
—William Glasser

One of the beauties of teaching is that there is no limit to one's growth as a teacher, just as there is no knowing beforehand how much your students can learn.

—HERBERT KOHL

Teaching is a rigorous act of faith.

—SUSAN OHANIAN, TEACHER

The one exclusive sign of thorough knowledge is the power of teaching.

—ARISTOTLE

Among the many purposes of schooling, four stand out to us as having special moral value: to love and care, to serve, to empower and, of course, to learn.
—Andy Hargreaves and Michael Fullan, from their book *What's Worth Fighting for Out There?* (1998)

Teaching is a calling, not a choice.
—Mary Ann Alexander, cosmetology teacher in Yorktown Heights, New York

Unfortunately, teaching is oftentimes like golf. So many bad shots in between the good. And those are the few shots that we need to remember.
—Howard Nero, fifth grade teacher from New Haven, Connecticut

15

Good teaching is primarily an art,
and can neither be defined or
standardized. . . . Good teachers are born
and made; neither part of the process can
be omitted.

—JOEL H. HILDEBRAND, IN AN INTERVIEW
CONDUCTED SHORTLY BEFORE HIS HUNDREDTH
BIRTHDAY

Hope and its twin, possibility, best describe
the art of teaching.

—CAMILLE BANKS-LEE, ENGLISH TEACHER IN OSSINING,
NEW YORK, 2002

Teaching is an exhausting job. I did not, however, expect to be emotionally exhausted. I suppose the easiest way out of this dilemma would be to make myself emotionally unavailable to my students . . . Not this teacher. This teacher can't help but share in some of those emotional moments. I can't turn off a portion of myself when I walk into the classroom. It's either the whole Mrs. Baer or nothing.

—ALLISON L. BAER, SIXTH GRADE TEACHER IN OHIO, AS QUOTED IN *WHAT TO EXPECT IN YOUR FIRST YEAR TEACHING* (1998)

Teaching is an instinctual art, mindful of potential, craving of realizations, a pausing, seamless process.
—A. BARTLETT GIAMATTI, FROM "THE AMERICAN TEACHER," *HARPER'S* (1980)

When the uncapped potential of a student meets the liberating art of a teacher, a miracle unfolds.
—MARY HATWOOD FUTRELL (1941–), DEAN AT GEORGE WASHINGTON UNIVERSITY

The basic idea behind teaching is to teach people what they need to know.
—CARL ROGERS

Teaching is the best way I know of regaining balance in your egocentric outlook on life.
—BARBARA GASPARIK, CHILD DEVELOPMENT TEACHER IN YORKTOWN HEIGHTS, NEW YORK, 2002

Teachers are the last bastion against darkness and ignorance. The intensity of this need was my surprise.
—JAMES W. MORRIS, FIFTH GRADE TEACHER FROM GEORGIA, QUOTED IN *WHAT TO EXPECT YOUR FIRST YEAR OF TEACHING* (1998)

Teaching is the most inherently hopeful act that I know of.
—PATRICIA MURPHY, TEACHER FROM OTTAWA, QUOTED IN *WHAT'S WORTH FIGHTING FOR OUT THERE?* (1998)

Teachers, I believe, are the most responsible and important members of society because their professional efforts affect the fate of the earth.
—HELEN CALDICOTT

One good teacher in a lifetime may sometimes change a delinquent into a solid citizen.
—PHILIP WYLIE

A teacher affects eternity. He can never tell where his influence stops.
—HENRY ADAMS

My heart is singing for joy this morning. A miracle has happened! The light of understanding has shone upon my little pupil's mind, and behold, all things are changed.
—ANNE SULLIVAN, TUTOR TO HELEN KELLER

In an effective classroom, students should not only know what they are doing, they should also know why and how.
—HARRY WONG, AUTHOR OF *THE FIRST DAYS OF SCHOOL*

I teach, therefore I am.
—ANONYMOUS

Never doubt that a small group of thoughtful, committed citizens can change the world. Indeed, it's the only thing that ever has.
—MARGARET MEAD

Getting things done is not always what is most important. There is value in allowing others to learn, even if the task is not accomplished as quickly, efficiently, or effectively.
—R.D. CLYDE

Moral education, as I understand it, is not about inculcating obedience to law or cultivating self-virtue, it is rather about finding within us an ever-increasing sense of the worth of creation. It is about how we can develop and deepen our intuitive sense of beauty and creativity.
—ANDREW LINZEY, ANIMAL RIGHTS ACTIVIST

One good schoolmaster is worth a thousand priests.
—ROBERT GREEN INGERSOLL

We are born weak, we have need of help; we are born destitute of everything, we stand in need of assistance; we are born stupid, we have need of understanding. All that we are not possessed of at our birth, and which we require when we grow up, is bestowed on us by education

—JEAN JACQUES ROUSSEAU

I believe that education is all about being excited about something. Seeing passion and enthusiasm helps push an educational message.

—STEVE IRWIN, THE CROCODILE HUNTER

There are two kinds of teachers: the kind that fill you with so much quail shot that you can't move, and the kind that just gives you a little prod behind and you jump to the skies.

—ROBERT FROST

To teach is to touch lives forever.

—ANONYMOUS

A poor surgeon hurts one person at a time. A poor teacher hurts 130.

—ERNEST L. BOYER

He that is taught only by himself has a fool for a master.

—BEN JONSON

The fact we must remember is that we are educating students for a world that will not be ours but will be theirs. Give them a chance to be heard.

—Dr. Carlos P. Romulo, Filipino diplomat, politician, soldier, journalist, and author

The first idea that the child must acquire, in order to be actively disciplined, is that of the difference between good and evil; and the task of the educator lies in seeing that the child does not confound good with immobility, and evil with activity.

—Maria Montessori

I think education is power. I think that being able to communicate with people is power. One of my main goals on the planet is to encourage people to empower themselves.

—OPRAH WINFREY

Teachers who inspire know that teaching is like cultivating a garden, and those who would have nothing to do with thorns must never attempt to gather flowers.

—ANONYMOUS

No one has yet fully realized the wealth of sympathy, kindness, and generosity hidden in the soul of a child. The effort of every true education should be to unlock that treasure.
—EMMA GOLDMAN (1869–1940), AKA "RED EMMA," LITHUANIAN-BORN ANARCHIST KNOWN FOR HER WRITINGS AND SPEECHES

I believe that every human soul is teaching something to someone nearly every minute here in mortality.
—M. RUSSELL BALLARD, MORMON LEADER

I touch the future. I teach.
—CHRISTA MCAULIFFE, TEACHER KILLED ON CHALLENGER SPACE SHUTTLE

Teacher: The child's third parent.

—Hyman Berston

Teaching kids to count is fine, but teaching them what counts is best.

—Bob Talbert

Good teaching is more a giving of right questions than a giving of right answers.

—Josef Albers

For every one of us that succeeds, it's because there's somebody there to show you the way out. The light doesn't always necessarily have to be in your family; for me it was teachers and school.

—Oprah Winfrey

The empires of the future are the empires of the mind.
—WINSTON CHURCHILL

Any genuine teaching will result, if successful, in someone's knowing how to bring about a better condition of things than existed earlier.
—JOHN DEWEY

Where there is an open mind there will always be a frontier.
—CHARLES F. KETTERING

Give me four years to teach the children and the seed I have sown will never be uprooted.
—VLADIMIR LENIN

Only the mind cannot be sent into exile.
—OVID

I know but one freedom, and that is the freedom of the mind.
—ANTOINE DE SAINT-EXUPERY

Education . . . is a painful, continual, and difficult work to be done in kindness, by watching, by warning . . . by praise, but above all, by example.
—JOHN RUSKIN

Men learn while they teach.
—LUCIUS A. SENECA

I put the relation of a fine teacher to a student just below the relation of a mother to a son.
—Thomas Wolfe

Life is an exciting business, and most exciting when it is lived for others.
—Helen Keller

Blessed is the influence of one true, loving human soul on another.
—George Eliot

'Tis education forms the common mind/Just as the twig is bent, the tree's inclined.
—Alexander Pope (1688–1744), from his collection of essays *Moral Essays: Epistle to Richard Boyle, Earl of Burlington*

31

The most important function of education at any level is to develop the personality of the individual and the significance of his life to himself and to others. This is the basic architecture of a life; the rest is ornamentation and decoration of the structure.

—GRAYSON KIRK

Those who educate children are more to be honored than those who produce them; for these only gave them life, those the art of living well.

—ARISTOTLE

Better than a thousand days of diligent study is one day with a great teacher.

—JAPANESE PROVERB

A human being is not attaining his full heights until he is educated.
—HORACE MANN

Events in our classrooms today will prompt world events tomorrow.
—J. LLOYD TRUMP, AS QUOTED IN *THE TEACHER AND THE TAUGHT* (1963)

He then learns that in going down into the secrets of his own mind he has descended into the secrets of all minds.
—RALPH WALDO EMERSON

Education is the jewel casting brilliance into the future.
—MARI EVANS

The whole object of education is . . . to develop the mind. The mind should be a thing that works.
—SHERWOOD ANDERSON

The utmost extent of man's knowledge is to know that he knows nothing.
—JOSEPH ADDISON, FROM *ESSAY ON PRIDE* (1794)

He who can, does. He who cannot, teaches.
—GEORGE BERNARD SHAW

Those who can't do, teach. Those who can't teach, teach gym.
—WOODY ALLEN

We make the road, others will make the journey.
—VICTOR HUGO, FROM HIS BOOK *THOUGHTS*, TRANSLATED IN 1907

Teaching gives me a greater sense of my own humanity.
—CAMILLE BANKS-LEE, ENGLISH TEACHER IN OSSINING, NEW YORK, 2002

Behold, I do not give lectures or a little charity/When I give I give myself.
—WALT WHITMAN

35

None of my other teachers held me up to the same standard as my English teacher, Ms. Tsang. I eventually learned to hold myself up to the same standard.

—Melissa Macomber, the Bancroft School class of 1989, 2002

I entered the classroom with the conviction that it was crucial for me and every other student to be an active participant, not a passive consumer . . . education that connects the will to know with the will to become.

—Bell Hooks, from his book *Teaching to Transgress* (1994)

I still felt the responsibility twenty-four hours a day! Teaching wasn't only my job, it was fast becoming my lifestyle.

—Scott D. Niemann, third and fourth grade teacher in Alaska, as quoted in *What to Expect Your First Year Teaching* (1998)

In our world of big names, curiously, our true heroes tend to be anonymous. In this life of illusion and quasi-illusion, the person of solid virtues who can be admired for something more substantial than his well-knownness often proves to be the unsung hero: the teacher, the nurse, the mother, the honest cop, the hard worker at lonely, underpaid, unglamorous, unpublicized jobs.

—Daniel J. Boorstin, from his book *The Image* (1961)

People snicker, "Those who can't do, teach." But, oh, how right they are. I could never, ever do all I dream of doing. I could never ever be an opera star, a baseball umpire . . . a great lover, a great liar, a trapeze artist, a writer, a dancer . . . or a thousand other aspirations I have had, while having only been given one thin ticket in this lottery of life!

—ESMÉ RAJI CODELL, FROM HER BOOK *EDUCATING ESMÉ* (1999)

Rosie, an autistic child, talks to me now and can say her name. Possibly she could have reached these milestones in another classroom, but it happened in mine. What greater joy can a teacher feel than to witness a child's success?

—MICHELLE L. GRAHAM, FIRST GRADE TEACHER IN MINNESOTA, AS QUOTED IN *WHAT TO EXPECT YOUR FIRST YEAR TEACHING* (1998)

It is written that he who governs well, leads the blind; but that he who teaches, gives them eyes.

—DAVID O. MCKAY, MORMON HUMANITARIAN AND EDUCATOR

I don't think we expect enough of students. There are a lot of fabulous young people out there. They just need someone to show them the way.

—Rafe Esquith, 1992 Disney Teacher of the Year and *Parent Magazine's* 1997 Teacher of the Year, from Hobart Boulevard Elementary School in Los Angeles, California

Most of us end up with no more than five or six people who remember us. Teachers have thousands of people who remember them for the rest of their lives.

—Andrew Rooney

I owe a lot to my teachers and mean to pay them back someday.

—Stephen Leacock

Jade best describes the art of teaching because it is the symbol of growth. As a teacher you must always find news ways of growing, and you must always strive to find new ways to help your students grow. Only in growth can the crop be harvested.

—Lylee Style, English teacher in Yorktown Heights, New York, 2002

Thirty-one chances. Thirty-one futures, our futures. It's an almost psychotic feeling, believing that part of their lives belongs to me. Everything they become, I also become. And everything about me, they helped to create.

—Esmé Raji Codell, from her book *Educating Esmé* (1999)

I am quite sure that in the hereafter she will take me by the hand and lead me to my proper seat.

—Bernard Baruch, on one of his early teachers in *News Summaries* (1955)

It's a vital thing to remember both as creative people and those who have the opportunity to nurture the creativity in others. Creativity requires courage!

—Thomas Kinkade

An education that does not strive to promote the fullest and most thorough understanding of the world is not worthy of the name.

—George S. Counts, as quoted in *The Teacher and the Taught* (1963)

The direction in which education starts a man will determine his future life.

—PLATO

Education is a kind of continuing dialogue, and a dialogue assumes . . . different points of view.

—ROBERT M. HUTCHINS, ON ACADEMIC FREEDOM IN *TIME*

The ability to think straight, some knowledge of the past, some vision of the future, some skill to do useful service, some urge to fit that service into the well-being of the community—these are the most vital things education must try to produce.

—VIRGINIA GILDERSLEEVE, FROM HER BOOK *MANY A GOOD CRUSADE* (1954)

To prepare for complete living is the function which education has to discharge; and the only rational mode of judging of an education course is, to judge in what degree it discharges such function.

—HERBERT SPENCER, FROM HIS ESSAY "ONE EDUCATION" (1859)

The need for imagination, as sense of truth, and a feeling of responsibility—these are the three forces which are the very nerve of education.

—RUDOLF STEINER

Teaching is what teachers expect to do every day. To reach out positively and supportively to twenty-seven youngsters for five hours or so each day in an elementary school classroom is demanding and exhausting. To respond similarly to four to six successive classes of twenty-four or more students each at the secondary level may be impossible.

—JOHN GOODARD, FROM HIS BOOK *A PLACE CALLED SCHOOL* (1984)

Human beings are full of emotion, and the teacher who knows how to use it will have dedicated learners. It means sending dominant signals instead of submissive ones with your eyes, body, and voice.

—LEON LESSINGER

In communities, the best disciplinary strategies are those that teach students citizenship and help students become caring adults. Key are the standards, values, and commitments that make up a constitution for living together.

—THOMAS J. SERGIOVANNI FROM HIS BOOK *BUILDING COMMUNITY IN SCHOOLS* (1994)

Children are liquid. They shape themselves to fit the form of the container into which they are placed . . . I am forever indebted to my teachers. They had enough faith to swing the bucket, because they knew that it was in the very nature of the water to remain right there.

—PAULA POLK LILLARD FROM HER BOOK *MONTESSORI TODAY: A COMPREHENSIVE APPROACH TO EDUCATION FROM BIRTH TO ADULTHOOD* (1996)

On a good day, I know it's not every day, we can part the sea/And on a bad day, I know it's not every day, glory beyond our reach.
—Chris Robinson, from his poem "Wiser Time" (1994)

I do not teach children, I give them joy.
—Isadora Duncan

No matter what accomplishments you achieve, somebody helped you.
—Althea Gibson

The influence of each human being on others in this life is a kind of immortality.
—Winston Churchill

A man who becomes conscious of the responsibility he bears toward a human being who affectionately waits for him, or to an unfinished work, will never be able to throw away his life. He knows the "why" for his existence, and will be able to bear almost any "how."
—Viktor Frankl, Austrian neurologist, psychiatrist, and Holocaust survivor

If you would thoroughly know anything, teach it to others.
—Tryon Edwards

Invest in a human soul. Who knows? It might be a diamond in the rough.
—MARY MCLEOD BETHUNE, EDUCATOR BORN TO FORMER SLAVE

It takes a city to raise a child.
—ADAIR LARA

Children are not born knowing the many opportunities that are theirs for the taking. Someone who does know must tell them.
—RUTH HILL VIGUERS, EDITOR OF *THE HORN BOOK* (1958–1967), FROM "RUTH HILL VIGUERS"

The best education is not given to students;
it is drawn out of them.
—GERALD BELCHER

The moment one gives close attention to
anything, even a blade of grass, it becomes
a mysterious, awesome, indescribably
magnificent world in itself.
—HENRY MILLER

There are two ways of spreading light;
to be the candle or the mirror that
reflects it.
—EDITH WHARTON

If you have knowledge, let others light their
candles in it.
—MARGARET FULLER

At the end of the visit, Diana reviews the events and the learning with the children. She asks the children their favorite event. "The alone walk," they all clamor. Walking all alone along the trail. Each one being brave, courageous. Discovering that they can find their own way.

—Lois Robin, referring to a schoolchildren's outing with Diana Almendariz, a Native American cultural interpreter descended from the Nisenan-Maidu tribe, from "A Day with Diana," Native California (1991)

When I transfer my knowledge, I teach. But when I transfer my beliefs, I indoctrinate.

—ARTHUR C. DANTO, FROM HIS BOOK *ANALYTICAL PHILOSOPHY OF KNOWLEDGE* (1968)

Teaching a solid subject such as English forced me to create a detailed schedule and lesson plan and to get things done efficiently without wasting time. I couldn't just amble into class each day without precise preparation.

—JOHN WOODEN

The great teachings unanimously emphasize that all the peace, wisdom, and joy in the universe are already within us; we don't have to gain, develop, or attain them. We're like a child standing in a beautiful park with his eyes shut tight. We don't need to imagine trees, flowers, deer, birds, and sky; we merely need to open our eyes and realize what is already here, who we really are. As soon as we quit pretending we're small or unholy.

—Anonymous

That in education we should proceed from the simple to the complex, is a truth which has always been to some extent acted upon: not professedly, indeed, nor any means consistently. The mind develops. Like all things that develop it progresses from the homogeneous to the heterogeneous; and a normal training system, being an objective counter-part of this subjective process, must exhibit a like progression.

—HERBERT SPENCER, FROM HIS ESSAY "INTELLECTUAL EDUCATION" (C. 1854)

I have come to believe that a great teacher is a great artist and that there are as few as there are any other great artists. Teaching might even be the greatest of the arts since the medium is the human mind and spirit.

—John Steinbeck

The teacher is just a boat to take the student over the river.

—Buddha

Upon our children—how they are taught—rests the fate—or fortune—of tomorrow's world.

—B. C. Forbes, financial journalist, author, and founder of Forbes magazine

It is noble to teach oneself; it is still nobler to teach others.

—Mark Twain

Education is the most powerful weapon which you can use to change the world.

—Nelson Mandela

Everyone and everything around you is your teacher.

—Ken Keyes, Jr.

I have come to a frightening conclusion. I am the decisive element in the classroom. It is my personal approach that creates the climate. It is my daily mood that makes the weather. As a teacher, I possess tremendous power to make a child's life miserable or joyous.

—Haim Ginott

56

The teacher's task is to initiate the learning process and then get out of the way.
—JOHN WARREN

I am that most fortunate of men for I am eternal. Others live merely in the world of today; I live in the world of tomorrow . . . For I am charged with that most sacred mission—to transmit all that our forebears lived for, loved for, and died for to the next generation.
—RABBI ZEV SCHOSTAK

The business of teaching is carried forward . . . because some individuals of extraordinary vitality and strength of personality engage in it and the fire that helps to guide them kindles the spirits of the young people whose lives they touch.
—WOODROW WILSON

A wise man knows and will keep his place; but a child is ignorant of his, and therefore cannot confine himself to it. There are a thousand avenues through which he will be apt to escape; it belongs to those who have the care of his education, therefore, to prevent him; a task, by the way, which is not very easy.
—JEAN JACQUES ROUSSEAU

It is one thing to show a man that he is in error, and another to put him in possession of truth.
—John Locke

To teach a man how he may learn to grow independently, and for himself, is the greatest service that one man can do another.
—Benjamin Jowett

If you can read this, thank a teacher.
—Anonymous

We cannot hold a torch to light another's path without brightening our own.
—Ben Sweetland

The critical factor is not class size but rather the nature of the teaching as it affects learning.

—C.B. Neblette

Education should turn out the pupil with something he knows well and something he can do well.

—Alfred North Whitehead

From what we get, we can make a living; what we give, however, makes a life.

—Arthur Ashe

Far and away the best prize that life offers is the chance to work hard at work worth doing.

—Theodore Roosevelt

The future of the world is in my classroom today, a future with the potential for good or bad.
—Ivan Welton Fitzwater

Education is helping the child realize his potentialities.
—Erich Fromm

Education is much more than a matter of imparting the knowledge and skills by which narrow goals are achieved. It is also about opening the child's eyes to the needs and rights of others.
—Dalai Lama

None of us got where we are solely by pulling ourselves up by our bootstraps. We got here because somebody—a parent, a teacher, an Ivy League crony or a few nuns, bent down and helped us pick up our boots.

—Thurgood Marshall

We make the best contribution in areas where our hearts call us to serve; and often these are areas where we have either a natural talent or interest.

—Thomas Kinkade

The beautiful compensation of developing favorable self-concepts in students is that the teacher cannot build positive self-concepts in students without building his own.

—WILLIAM PURKEY

The greater part of the people we assign to educate our children we know for certain are not educated. Yet we do not doubt that they can give what they have not received, a thing which cannot be otherwise acquired.

—GIACOMO LEOPARDI

No one has ever taught anything to anybody.

—CARL ROGERS

Teachers are people who start things they never see finished, and for which they never get thanks until it is too late.
—Max Forman

The vanity of teaching doth oft tempt a man to forget that he is a blockhead.
—George Savile, Marquis of Halifax (1633–1695), English statesman, and essayist

You don't have to think too hard when you talk to teachers.
—J.D. Salinger

One of the true tests of leadership is the ability to recognize a problem before it becomes an emergency.
—Arnold Glasow

The highest of distinctions is service to others.
—KING GEORGE VI

A leader is someone who helps improve the lives of other people or improve the system they live under.
—SAM ERVIN

The first duty of a lecturer—to hand you after an hour's discourse a nugget of pure truth to wrap up between the pages of your notebooks and keep on the mantelpiece for ever.
—VIRGINIA WOOLF

Forget committees. New, noble, world-changing ideas always come from one person working alone.
—H. Jackson Brown Jr., from his book *Life's Little Instruction Book* (2000)

The second most important job in the world, second only to being a good parent, is being a good teacher.
—S.G. Ellis

I cannot teach you; only help you to explore yourself.
—Bruce Lee

The world does not pay for what a person knows. But it pays for what a person does with what he knows.

—Laurence Lee

Great minds are to make others great. Their superiority is to be used, not to break the multitude to intellectual vassalage, not to establish over them a spiritual tyranny, but to rouse them from lethargy, and to aid them to judge for themselves.

—William Ellery Channing

Be all that you can be. Find your future—as a teacher.

—Madeline Fuchs Holzer, Arts in Education director for the New York State Council on the Arts

The first condition of education is being able to put someone to wholesome and meaningful work.
—John Ruskin

Your best teacher is your last mistake.
—Ralph Nader

When the student is ready the teacher will appear.
—Lao Tzu (c. 600 B.C.), Chinese philosopher, founder of Chinese Taoism, known as "Old Master"

He who dares to teach must never cease to learn.
—Anonymous

There's no word in the language I revere more than "teacher." My heart sings when a kid refers to me as his teacher, and it always has. I've honored myself and the entire family of man by becoming a teacher.

—Pat Conroy, from his book *Prince of Tides* (1986)

We live in a time of such rapid change and growth of knowledge that only he who is in a fundamental sense a scholar—that is, a person who continues to learn and inquire—can hope to keep pace, let alone play the role of guide.

—Nathan M. Pusey, from his book *The Age of the Scholar* (1963)

My first year has been as disappointing as it was rewarding . . . I have lost and found hope, reviewed and revised, and finally concluded that my presence here is much more important that I had thought it would be.

—Catherine McTamaney, high school teacher from Tennessee, as quoted in *What to Expect Your First Year Teaching* (1998)

I have been maturing as a teacher. New experiences bring new sensitivities and flexibility.

—Howard Lester, first-year teacher

Creativity does not exist on a continuum. Rather, there are small groups of teachers in every school that work in unique systems.
—Jim Schulz, 2000 Disney Teacher of the Year, from Helena, Montana

But the first day of school is our second New Year's. It is our day to make resolutions, to look backward to former lapses and triumphs and to look ahead, usually with a mix of anxiety and hope, to the year to come.
—Mark Edmundon, from "Soul Training," *The New York Times Magazine* (2002)

Choose a job you love, and you will never have to work a day in your life.
—Confucius

Philosophy lies deeper. It is not her office to teach men how to use their hands. The object of her lessons is to form the soul.
—LUCIUS A. SENECA, FROM HIS BOOK *EPISTULAE AND LUCILIUM* (A.D. 63)

I don't know what your destiny will be, but one thing I know: the only ones among you who will be truly happy are those who will have sought and found how to serve.
—ALBERT SCHWEITZER

It is nobler to be good, and it is nobler to teach others to be good— and less trouble!
—MARK TWAIN

I'm not a teacher: only a fellow-traveler of whom you asked the way. I pointed ahead—ahead of myself as well as you.
—GEORGE BERNARD SHAW

There were great frustrations, setbacks, and embarrassing moments, but the pleasure of teaching young people was more than money could buy.
—JOHN WOODEN, FROM HIS BOOK *MY PERSONAL BEST* (2004)

A professor can never better distinguish himself in his work than by encouraging a clever pupil, for the true discoverers are among them, as comets amongst the stars.
—CAROLUS LINNAEUS

True undoubting is the teacher's part,
continual undoubting the part of the pupil.
—Franz Kafka

Painter Marc Chagall is my favorite pupil and
what I like about him is that after listening
attentively to my lessons he takes his paints
and brushes and does something absolutely
different from what I have told him.
—Leon Bakst

We Teach Success
—Hofstra University advertising slogan

Any activity becomes creative when the doer cares about doing it right, or doing it better.
—John Updike

A classic lecture, rich in sentiment, With scraps of thunderous epic lilted out By violet-hooded Doctors, elegies And quoted odes, and jewels five-words long, That on the stretched forefinger of all Time Sparkle for ever.
—Alfred Lord Tennyson, from his book *The Princess* (1847)

Few have been taught to any purpose who have not been their own teachers.
—Sir Joshua Reynolds

The Lord & the teacher face me. Who should I kneel before? I pay my obeisance to you, my teacher, since you took me to the Lord.
—Sufi Saint Kabir, Indian mystic

Those who live life for themselves will be stuck with themselves—and little else.
—Thomas Kinkade

And just as I've always wanted our players to be a part of the student body, so too have I always wanted our students to be a part of our team. And I think that our students have been that.
—Bobby Knight

The most dangerous leadership myth is that leaders are born—that there is a genetic factor to leadership. This myth asserts that people simply either have certain charismatic qualities or not. That's nonsense; in fact, the opposite is true. Leaders are made rather than born.

—WARREN G. BENNIS

There is nothing training cannot do. Nothing is above its reach. It can turn bad morals to good; it can destroy bad principles and recreate good ones; it can lift men to angel-ship.

—MARK TWAIN

No matter what your product is, you are ultimately in the education business. Your customers need to be constantly educated about the many advantages of doing business with you, trained to use your products more effectively, and taught how to make never-ending improvement in their lives.

—ROBERT G. ALLEN

Every truth has four corners: as a teacher I give you one corner, and it is for you to find the other three.

—CONFUCIUS

What the teacher is is more important than what he teaches.

—KARL MENNINGER

The teacher as a person is more important than the teacher as a technician. What he is has more effect than anything he does.

—JACK CANFIELD

Wherever there are beginners and experts, old and young, there is some kind of learning going on, some kind of teaching. We are all pupils and we are all teachers.

—GILBERT HIGHET

THE PHILOSOPHY
BEHIND GOOD
TEACHING

It's what you learn after you know it all that counts.

—EARL WEAVER

Who dares to teach, must never cease to learn.

—JOHN COTTON DANA

What is important is to keep learning, to enjoy challenge, and to tolerate ambiguity. In the end there are no certain answers.

—MARTINA HORNER

Instruction begins when you, the teacher, learn from the learner; put yourself in his place so that you may understand . . . what he learns and the way he understands it.

—SØREN KIERKEGAARD

Acquire new knowledge whilst thinking over the old, and you may become a teacher of others.

—CONFUCIUS

The teacher who is indeed wise Does not bid you to enter the house of his wisdom But rather leads you to the threshold of your mind.

—KAHLIL GIBRAN, FROM HIS BOOK *THE PROPHET* (1923)

The best teacher is the one who suggests rather than dogmatizes, and inspires his listener with the wish to teach himself.

—EDWARD BULWER-LYTTON

The mediocre teacher tells. The good teacher explains. The superior teacher demonstrates. The great teacher inspires.
—WILLIAM ARTHUR WARD

Patience is the key to paradise.
—ARMENIAN PROVERB

Patience is the companion of wisdom.
—ST. AUGUSTINE

Have a heart that never hardens, and a temper that never fires, and a touch that never hurts.
—CHARLES DICKENS

Many of us carry memories of an influential teacher who may scarcely know we existed, yet who said something at just the right time in our lives to snap a whole world into focus.

—Laurent A. Daloz

One looks back with appreciation to the brilliant teachers, but with gratitude to those who touched our human feeling. The curriculum is so much necessary raw material, but warmth is the vital element for the growing plant and for the soul of the child.

—Carl Jung

They may forget what you said but they will never forget how you made them feel.

—Anonymous

Your heart is slightly bigger than the average human heart, but that's because you're a teacher.
—Aaron Bacall

You can pay people to teach, but you can't pay them to care.
—Marva Collins, from her book *Making a Difference in the Classroom* (1992)

A word of encouragement during a failure is worth more than an hour of praise after success.
—Anonymous

To waken interest and kindle enthusiasm is the sure way to teach easily and successfully.
—Tyron Edwards

No man can be a good teacher unless he has feelings of warm affection toward his pupils and a genuine desire to impart to them what he himself believes to be of value.

—Bertrand Russell

A word as to the education of the heart. We don't believe that this can be imparted through books; it can only be imparted through the loving touch of the teacher.

—César Chávez

Teachers believe they have a gift for giving; it drives them with the same irrepressible drive that drives others to create a work of art or a marker or a building.

—A. BARTLETT GIAMATTI, FORMER PRESIDENT OF YALE UNIVERSITY

Too often we underestimate the power of a touch, a smile, a kind word, a listening ear, an honest compliment, or the smallest act of caring, all of which have the potential to turn a life around.

—DR. LEO BUSCAGLIA

The close observer soon discovers that the teacher's task is not to implant facts but to place the subject to be learned in front of the learner and, through sympathy, emotion, imagination, and patience, to awaken in the learner the restless drive for answers and insights which enlarge the personal life and give it meaning.

—Nathan M. Pusey

A teacher who is attempting to teach, without inspiring the pupil with a desire to learn, is hammering on a cold iron.

—Horace Mann

The task of the excellent teacher is to stimulate "apparently ordinary" people to unusual effort. The tough problem is not in identifying winners: it is in making winners out of ordinary people.

—K. Patricia Cross

The test of a good teacher is not how many questions he can ask his pupils that they will answer readily, but how many questions he inspires them to ask him which he finds it hard to answer.

—Alice Wellington Rollins

Teaching is not a profession; it's a passion.

—Anonymous

No one should teach who is not in love with teaching.
—Margaret E. Sangster

The gift of teaching is a peculiar talent, and implies a need and a craving in the teacher himself.
—John Jay Chapman

There is no real teacher who in practice does not believe in the existence of the soul, or in a magic that acts on it through speech.
—Allan Bloom

Conviction is worthless unless it is converted to conduct.
—Thomas Carlyle

A good teacher is a master of simplification and an enemy of simplism.
—Louis A. Berman

To know how to suggest is the great art of teaching. To attain it we must be able to guess what will interest; we must learn to read the childish soul as we might a piece of music. Then, by simply changing the key, we keep up the attraction and vary the song.
—Henri-Frédéric Amiel, from his memoir *Journal in Time* (1864)

Setting an example is not the main means of influencing another, it is the only means.
—Albert Einstein

Example is the school of mankind, and they will learn at no other.
—Edmund Burke

Children have more need of models than critics.
—Joseph Joubert

Those who trust us educate us.
—George Eliot

The secret of education is respecting the pupil.
—Ralph Waldo Emerson

Love them enough to risk their not liking you. Children must know that there are consequences to be suffered when they are not nice.

—Carol Avila, teacher from Rhode Island and 1995 Presidential Award winner for Excellence in Science Teaching.

Patience is the greatest of all virtues.

—Dionysius Cato

Beware the fury of a patient man.

—John Dryden

Patience, that blending of moral courage with physical timidity.

—Thomas Hardy

Lack o' pep is often mistaken for patience.
—Kin Hubbard

Patience is necessary, and one cannot reap immediately where one has sown.
—Søren Kierkegaard

You have to have a lot of patience to learn patience.
—Stanislaw J. Lec

Patience, the beggar's virtue.
—Philip Massinger, from his book *A New Way to Pay Old Debts* (1631)

Nothing comes of so many things, if you have patience.
—Joyce Carol Oates

Patience and Diligence, like Faith, move Mountains.
—William Penn, from his book *Some Fruits of Solitude* (1693)

All's well in the end, if you've only the patience to wait.
—François Rabelais, from his book *Gargantua and Pantagrue* (1532–1552)

It is very strange . . . that the years teach us patience; that the shorter our time, the greater our capacity for waiting.
—Elizabeth Taylor

Patience doesn't always help, but impatience never does.
—RUSSIAN PROVERB

A good teacher is one who helps you become who you feel yourself to be. A good teacher is also one who says something that you won't understand until 10 years later.
—JULIUS LESTER

The teacher is one who made two ideas grow where only one grew before.
—ELBERT HUBBARD

The true teacher defends his pupils against his own personal influence. He inspires self-distrust. He guides their eyes from himself to the spirit that quickens him. He will have no disciple.

—Amos Bronson Alcott

That is the difference between good teachers and great teachers: good teachers make the best of a pupil's means; great teachers foresee a pupil's ends.

—Maria Callas

Effective teachers seek feedback and consensus on their decisions and make sure that students understand.

—Linda Shalaway

A wise teacher makes learning a joy.
—ANONYMOUS

The most effective teacher will always be
biased, for the chief force in teaching is
confidence and enthusiasm.
—JOYCE CARY

An understanding heart is everything
in a teacher, and cannot be esteemed
highly enough.
—CARL JUNG

The best teacher is one who suggests rather
than dogmatizes, and inspires his listener
with the wish to teach himself.
—ANONYMOUS

He that teaches us anything which we knew not before is undoubtedly to be reverenced as a master.
—Samuel Johnson

A good teacher is like a candle—it consumes itself to light the way for others.
—Anonymous

A great teacher is one who possesses information, intelligence, and the instincts to know how to present what he knows.
—Socrates

The gift of a great teacher is creating an awareness of greatness in others.
—Greta K. Nagel, from her book *The Tao of Teaching* (1998)

A good teacher is one who can understand those who are not very good at explaining, and explain to those who are not very good at understanding.
—Dwight D. Eisenhower

Inspired teachers . . . cannot be ordered by the gross from the factory. They must be discovered one by one, and brought home from the woods and swamps like orchids. They must be placed in a conservatory, not in a carpenter shop; and they must be honored and trusted.
—John Jay Chapman

Have you ever really had a teacher? One who saw you as a raw but precious thing, a jewel that, with wisdom, could be polished to a proud shine?

—MITCH ALBOM, FROM HIS BOOK *TUESDAYS WITH MORRIE* (1997)

A good teacher is never done with their preparation—grading, evaluations, planning—because they are always trying to reinvent, improve, and inspire.

—DR. DAVID CARLSON

Endeavor first, to broaden your children's sympathies and, but satisfying their daily needs, to bring love and kindness into such unceasing contact with their impressions and their activity, that these sentiments may be engrafted in their hearts.

—Johann Heinrich Pestalozzi

There are a number of teachers I wouldn't mind buying a drink, but precious few I'd like to sit and talk with while they drink it.

—Greg MacGilpin, Teacher's College of Columbia University

Experienced teachers . . . are an invaluable resource to the first-year teachers who are willing to admit that they have much to learn.
—ROBERT GRESS, TEACHER FROM LEXINGTON, KENTUCKY

Compassionate teachers fill a void left by working parents who aren't able to devote enough attention to their children. A good education consists of much more than useful facts and marketable skills.
—CHARLES PLATT

You can't stop a teacher when they want to do something. They just do it.
—J.D. SALINGER, FROM HIS BOOK *THE CATCHER IN THE RYE* (1951)

104

I was still learning when I taught my last class.
—CLAUDE M. FUESS

A great teacher never strives to explain his vision. He simply invites you to stand beside him and see for yourself.
—REVEREND E. INMAN

There is humane aggression in being a great teacher, as well as genuine love.
—MARK EDMUNDSON, FROM "SOUL TRAINING," *THE NEW YORK TIMES MAGAZINE* (2002)

To be a teacher in the right sense is to be a learner. I am not a teacher, only a fellow student.
—SØREN KIERKEGAARD

Good teachers must primarily be enthusiasts like writers, painters and priests, they must have a sense of vocation—a deep-rooted unsentimental desire to do good.

—NOEL COWARD

A teacher is one who makes himself progressively unnecessary.

—THOMAS CARRUTHERS

I like a teacher who gives you something to take home to think about besides homework.

—LILY TOMLIN

A professor is one who talks in someone else's sleep.

—ANONYMOUS

Good teachers are those who know how little they know. Bad teachers are those who think they know more than they don't know.
—R. VERDI

The most extraordinary thing about a really good teacher is that he or she transcends accepted educational methods. Such methods are designed to help average teachers approximate the performance of good teachers.
—MARGARET MEAD

Good teachers empathize with kids, respect them, and believe that each one has something special that can be built upon.
—ANN LIEBERMAN

If ever there can be a cause worthy to be upheld by all toil or sacrifice that the human heart can endure, it is the cause of education.
—Horace Mann

What greater or better gift can we offer the republic than to teach and instruct our youth?
—Marcus T. Cicero

A good teacher must be able to put himself in the place of those who find learning hard.
—Eliphas Levi, French occultist

Teachers teach because they care. Teaching young people is what they do best. It requires long hours, patience, and care.
—Horace Mann

We think of the effective teachers we have had over the years with a sense of recognition, but those who have touched our humanity we remember with a deep sense of gratitude.
—ANONYMOUS

Joe Rinaldi changed his teaching style to meet the student's learning needs. He never got frustrated when you didn't "get it." Instead, he changed the way he explained it.
—DEBBIE SABATO, FOURTH GRADE TEACHER IN DENVER, COLORADO

I love to feel proud: proud of a child who learns the English language, proud of a child who makes the perfect M, proud of a child who acts like a friend and can be a model for the class, proud of a child who learns his or her line for the school play.
—Karen Guardino, kindergarten teacher in Scarsdale, New York

Fifteen years after I sat on the big cozy rug in her kindergarten classroom, Ms. Cerbone remembered my name, the bows I used to wear in my hair, the dresses that my mom made for me. Each time we ran into each other, she would recall the memories with a smile. She never forgot.
—Kim Walkley Buckley, Bedford Hills Elementary School class of 1981

Each of Dr. Dominquez's classes were intense and draining, but worthwhile. He was the one teacher I could go to for advice and trust that I would get an honest answer.

—Suzie DeRoberts, Harvard University class of 1996

The best teachers teach from the heart, not from the book.

—Anonymous

I still can not get used to how much my heart soars with every student's success, and how a piece of my heart is plucked away when any student slips away.

—Delissa L. Mai, ninth grade teacher in Wyoming, as quoted in *What to Expect in Your First Year of Teaching* (1998)

Before I grew out of my shell, Ms. Sartor knew how shy I was. She wouldn't make me speak in front of the other students. Later, though, she would ask me questions, one-on-one.
—WENDY JACKSON, WESTON ELEMENTARY SCHOOL CLASS OF 1981

Professor Rimmerman would bleed red ink all over your paper. You still might eke out a B, but he would definitely let you know what to work on next time around.
—MARVIN T. LAO, HOBART COLLEGE CLASS OF 1994

Ms. Kennedy taught me to love writing. Every story came back with a smiley face at the top of the page.
—JOHN MCEDELMAN, BEDFORD VILLAGE ELEMENTARY SCHOOL CLASS OF 1981

Ms. Tulin was funny, laid back, kind of funky. She allowed you to be a teenager but also demanded respect and order in the classroom. We learned about the Holocaust, survival in the wilderness, ourselves . . . and she was wonderful at facilitating all of this.
—CARRIE PECK, FOX LANE MIDDLE SCHOOL CLASS OF 1985

I determined that there should not be a minute in the day when my children should not be aware of my face and my lips that my heart was theirs, that their happiness was my happiness, and their pleasures my pleasures.
—JOHANN HEINRICH PESTALOZZI, AS QUOTED IN THE TEACHER AND THE TAUGHT (1963)

Mr. Shanley's kindness put me at ease and gave me confidence to learn. It's hard to absorb information when your brain is congested with doubt, and his encouragement helped me to relax and, in turn, to excel academically. He's the one I will remember because he's the one who seemed to care.

—MEREDITH McWADE, FOX LANE HIGH SCHOOL CLASS OF 1989

Ms. Lambert gave us quizzes every day, not just as a way of dipsticking our understanding but as a means of evaluating her own clarity in teaching. I've never been so prepared for a class in my life.

—SUZIE DeROBERTS, FOX LANE HIGH SCHOOL CLASS OF 1992

Mr. Ehrhard was so interesting that you absolutely wanted to share in everything he cared about. He was the physics teacher who recommended *The Catcher in the Rye* and we all read it, of our own free will.

—ALICIA SOLÍS, WESTON HIGH SCHOOL CLASS OF 1990

I must have talked a great deal because Martha used to say again and again, "You remember you said this, you said that . . ." She remembered everything I said, and all my life I've had the feeling that what I think and what I say are worth remembering. She gave me that.

—ERIC HOFFER, ON MARTHA BAUER, THE WOMAN WHO RAISED HIM AFTER HIS MOTHER DIED, FROM "PROFILES: THE CREATIVE SITUATION," THE *NEW YORKER* (1967)

Teachers who really value their emotional bonds to students are willing to experiment with alternative structures that make these bonds stronger.
—Andy Hargreaves and Michael Fullan, from their book *What's Worth Fighting for Out There?* (1998)

Gladly would he learn and gladly teach.
—Geoffrey Chaucer, on the Clerk in his book *The Canterbury Tales*

The ultimate leader is one who is willing to develop people to the point that they eventually surpass him or her in knowledge and ability.
—Fred A. Manske, Jr.

A good coach will make his players see what they can be rather than what they are.

—ARA PARASEGHIAN

The test of a good coach is that when they leave, others will carry on successfully.

—ANONYMOUS

Outstanding leaders go out of their way to boost the self-esteem of their personnel. If people believe in themselves, it's amazing what they can accomplish.

—SAM WALTON

The boss drives people; the leader coaches them . . . The boss inspires fear; the leader inspires enthusiasm. The boss says "I"; the leader says "WE". The boss fixes the blame for the breakdown; the leader fixes the breakdown. The boss says, "GO"; the leader says, "Let's GO!"
—H. Gordon Selfridge

It is the greatest achievement of a teacher to enable his students to surpass him.
—John Kemeny

Terry Culleton made that impact on me. "If you want a future in writing, I think you've got it," he wrote on one paper. "If you're willing to try."

—Keith Dixon, George School class of 1989

The man who can make hard things easy is the educator.

—Ralph Waldo Emerson

I asked a student one day why he thought he was doing so much better than last year. He gave meaning to my whole new orientation. "It's because I like myself now when I'm with you," he said.

—Anonymous teacher, as quoted by Everett Shostrom in *Man, the Manipulator* (1968)

Do not train children to learning by force and harshness; but direct them to it by what amuses their minds, so that you may be better able to discover with accuracy the peculiar bent of the genius of each.
—PLATO

Education should be gentle and stern, not cold and lax.
—JOSEPH JOUBERT

As a teacher I feel I have a moral obligation to help the children in my classroom grow toward becoming full human beings and to feel successful. Teaching cognitive skills is not enough.
—JEAN MEDICK

Don't set your wit against a child.
—JONATHAN SWIFT

No use to shout at them to pay attention. If the situations, the materials, the problems before the child do not interest him, his attention will slip off to what does interest him, and no amount of exhortation of threats will bring him back.
—HENRY HOLT

People's behavior makes sense if you think about it in terms of their goals, needs, and motives.
—THOMAS MANN

WORDS FROM
THE WISE

If I compliment them, I mean it. If I don't think they are doing a good job, I lay it on the line. I demand respect from them and I give them respect, and I think they are important.
—Lenni Abel, Art teacher and 2000 Disney Teacher of the Year, from the Bronx, New York

I let the kids know exactly what I expect. I praise them when they meet those expectations and point it out to them when they don't.
—Ron Clark, fifth grade teacher and 2000 Disney Teacher of the Year, from Harlem, New York

The more you prepare outside of class, the less you perspire in class. The less you perspire in class, the more you inspire the class.
—HO BOON TIONG

If a child can't learn the way we teach, maybe we should teach the way they learn.
—IGNACIO ESTRADA

A teacher should have maximal authority, and minimal power.
—THOMAS SZASZ

Don't try to fix the students, fix ourselves first. The good teacher makes the poor student good and the good student superior. When our students fail, we, as teachers, too, have failed.

—Marva Collins, from her book *Making a Difference in the Classroom* (1992)

Treat the students the way you would want to be treated.

—Anonymous

Teachers should guide without dictating, and participate without dominating.

—C.B. Neblette

Remember that you are a teacher; you are helping people, making them feel safer, taking them from fear to love, from ignorance to knowledge.
—STUART WILDE

A schoolmaster should have an atmosphere of awe, and walk wonderingly, as if he was amazed at being himself.
—WALTER BAGEHOT

If the teacher is not respected and the student not cared for, confusion will arise, however clever one is.
—LAO TZU

All kids need is a little help, a little hope and somebody who believes in them.
—EARVIN "MAGIC" JOHNSON

Nothing you do for children is ever wasted.
—GARRISON KEILLOR

A teacher ought, therefore, to be as agreeable as possible, that remedies, which are rough in their nature, may be rendered soothing by gentleness of hand; he ought to praise some parts of his pupils' performances, tolerate some, and to alter others, giving his reasons why the alterations are made.
—QUINTILIAN

Learning must never be imposed as a Task, nor made a Trouble to them. There may be Dice and Playthings with the Letters on them to teach Children the Alphabet by playing; and twenty other Ways may be found, suitable to their particular Tempers, to make this kind of Learning a Sport to them.

—JOHN LOCKE, FROM HIS BOOK *SOME THOUGHTS CONCERNING EDUCATION AND OF THE CONDUCT OF THE UNDERSTANDING* (1693)

One of the most important things a teacher can do is to send the pupil home in the afternoon liking himself just a little better than when he came in that morning.

—ERNEST MELBY, COMMUNITY EDUCATOR ADVOCATE

You can't teach people everything they need to know. The best you can do is position them where they can find what they need to know when they need to know it.

—Seymour Papert

Never tell a young person that something cannot be done. God may have been waiting for centuries for somebody ignorant enough of the impossibility to do that thing.

—Dr. J. A. Holmes

The finest gift you can give anyone is encouragement. Yet, almost no one gets the encouragement they need to grow to their full potential. If everyone received the encouragement they need to grow, the genius in most everyone would blossom and the world would produce abundance beyond our wildest dreams.

—SIDNEY MADWED

Never tell people how to do things. Tell them what to do and they will surprise you with their ingenuity.

—GEORGE PATTON

Teaching high school, in addition to knowing one's subject matter thoroughly and being able to convey it to others, requires the grit of a long-distance runner, the stamina of a boxer going fifteen rounds, the temperament of a juggler and the street smarts of a three-card Monte dealer.

—Professor Larry Cuban

We think it's about little techniques and tricks, but techniques only take you so far. We need teachers who care about kids, who care about what they teach, and who can communicate with kids.

—Parker J. Palmer, from his book *The Courage to Teach* (1997)

Whatever you want to teach, be brief.
—HORACE

It would be a great advantage to some
schoolmasters if they would steal two hours
a day from their pupils, and give their own
minds the benefit of the robbery.
—J. F. BOYSE

Every leader needs to remember that
a healthy respect for authority takes
time to develop. It's like building
trust. You don't instantly have trust,
it has to be earned.
—MIKE KRZYZEWSKI, COLLEGE BASKETBALL
COACH

The job of an educator is to teach students to see the vitality in themselves.

—Joseph Campbell

Life is amazing: and the teacher had better prepare himself to be a medium for that amazement.

—Edward Blishen

Learn in order to teach and to practice.

—Talmud Rabbinical writings

Instruction begins when you, the teacher, learn from the learner; put yourself in his place so that you may understand . . . what he learns and the way he understands it.

—Søren Kierkegaard

Acquire new knowledge whilst thinking over the old, and you may become a teacher of others.

—CONFUCIUS

Patience is the key to paradise.

—ARMENIAN PROVERB

Patience is the companion of wisdom.
—ST. AUGUSTINE

A teacher's purpose is not to create students in his own image, but to develop students who can create their own image.

—ANONYMOUS

Creative minds have always been known to survive any kind of bad training.
—Anna Freud

A teacher who is attempting to teach, without inspiring the pupil with a desire to learn, is hammering on a cold iron.
—Horace Mann

Give the pupils something to do, not something to learn; and the doing is of such a nature as to demand thinking; learning naturally results.
—John Dewey

Merely to stuff the child with a lot of information, making him pass examinations, is the most unintelligent form of education.
—Jiddu Krishnamurti

Spoon feeding in the long run teaches us nothing but the shape of the spoon.
—*The Observer*, "Sayings of the Week," October 7, 1951

Seek help. Always question us veteran teachers and we will find the answers together.
—Carol Avila, teacher from Rhode Island and 1995 Presidential Award winner for Excellence in Science Teaching

The teacher's task is not to implant facts but to place the subject to be learned in front of the learner and, through sympathy, emotion, imagination and patience, to awaken in the learner the restless drive for answers and insights which enlarge the personal life and give it meaning.
—Nathan M. Pusey

"Aliveness" in the teacher must pass over to "aliveness" in the children.
—Rudolf Steiner

If in any manner we can stimulate the higher form of knowing, new passages are opened for us into nature; the mind flows into and through things hardest and highest and metamorphosis is possible.

—Ralph Waldo Emerson

Three things give the student the possibility of surpassing his teacher: ask a lot of questions, remember the answers, teach.

—Jan Amos Coménius

Teachers must regard every imperfection in the pupil's comprehension not as a defect but as a deficit in his or her own instruction, and endeavor to develop the ability to discover a new method of teaching.
—LEO TOLSTOY

If you become a teacher, by your pupils you'll be taught.
—OSCAR HAMMERSTEIN II

There is nothing more unequal than the equal treatment of unequal people.
—THOMAS JEFFERSON

Mentoring is all about people—it's about caring, about relationships and sensitivity. As it becomes increasingly in vogue it is becoming too formulated—concerned with performance metrics, critical success factors, investment, and spending. It'll be a disaster.

—RENE CARAYOL, BUSINESS GURU

You teach best what you most need to learn.

—RICHARD BACH

The lecturer should give the audience full reason to believe that all his powers have been exerted for their pleasure and instruction.

—MICHAEL FARADAY

Theories and goals of education don't matter a whit if you do not consider your students to be human beings.
—Lou Ann Walker

When love and skill work together, expect a masterpiece.
—John Ruskin

A man should first direct himself in the way he should go. Only then should he instruct others.
—Buddha

Everything should be made as simple as possible, but not simpler.
—Albert Einstein

To arrive at the simple is difficult.
—Rashid Elisha

Being entirely honest with oneself is a good exercise.
—Sigmund Freud

The way to gain a good reputation is to endeavor to be what you desire to appear.
—Socrates

These children taught me a very simple but often overlooked principle. Believe in a child's power to succeed and they will succeed.
—Maggie Keyser, 1999 Disney Teacher of the Year, from Lafayette Elementary School

The teaching goes on.
—MITCH ALBOM, FROM HIS BOOK *TUESDAYS WITH MORRIE* (1997)

Sometimes the last thing learners need is for their preferred learning style to be affirmed. Agreeing to let people learn only in a way that feels comfortable and familiar can restrict seriously their chance for development.
—STEPHEN BROOKFIELD

I was always prepared for success, but that means that I have to be prepared for failure, too.
—SHEL SILVERSTEIN

One of the least discussed ways of carrying a student through a hard unit of material is to challenge him with a change to exercise his full powers, so that he may discover the pleasure of full and effective functioning.

—Jerome S. Bruner, as quoted in *The Teacher and the Taught* (1963)

We must beware of what I will call "inert ideas" that is to say, ideas that are merely received into the mind without being utilized or tested or thrown into fresh combinations.

—Alfred North Whitehead, from his book *Aims of Education and Other Essays* (1967)

Our highest endeavor must be to develop free human beings, who are able of themselves to impart purpose and direction to their lives.

—RUDOLF STEINER

Only that which does not teach, which does not cry out, which does not persuade, which does not condescend, which does not explain, is irresistible.

—W. B. YEATS

The mind, like the body, cannot assimilate beyond a certain rate; and if you ply it with facts faster than it can assimilate them, they are soon rejected again: instead of being built into the intellectual fabric, they fall out of recollection after the passing of the examination for which they were got up.
—HERBERT SPENCER

As teachers, we must constantly try to improve schools and we must keep working at changing and experimenting and trying until we have developed ways of teaching every child.
—ALBERT SHANKER

Teaching consists of causing people to go into situations from which they cannot escape, except by thinking. Do not handicap your children by making their lives easy.

—ROBERT HEINLEIN, FROM HIS BOOK *THE NOTEBOOKS OF LAZARUS LONG* (1973)

You need to have a plan of sorts, but don't become consumed by it. Winds change.

—JOSEPH EHRHARD, PHYSICS TEACHER FROM WESTON, CONNECTICUT

Teachers who get "burned out" are not the ones who are constantly learning, which can be exhilarating, but those who feel they must stay in control and ahead of the students at all times.

—FRANK SMITH

Few things help an individual more than to place responsibility upon him, and to let him know that you trust him.

—Booker T. Washington

When angry, count to ten, before you speak; if very angry, an hundred.

—Thomas Jefferson, in a letter to Thomas Jefferson Smith (1825)

The benefits gained from learning how to manage conflict constructively far outweighs the costs of learning time lost by students being upset and angry.

—Thomas J. Sergiovanni, from his book *Building Community in Schools* (1994)

When I taught in public high school for three years I always ate lunch with a different group of students whether they were in my class or not, until I got to know most of them. The teachers thought I was idiotic, but they didn't realize that it actually made it easier for me to teach, that before I could effectively discipline students, I had to earn their friendship and respect.

—MARVA COLLINS, FROM HER BOOK *MAKING A DIFFERENCE IN THE CLASSROOM* (1992)

You can preach at them: that is a hook without a worm; you can order them to volunteer: that is dishonest; you can call upon them: you are needed, and that approach will hardly ever fail.

—KURT HAHN, AS QUOTED IN *RECLAIMING YOUTH AT RISK: OUR HOPE FOR THE FUTURE* (1990)

Children may forget what you say, but they'll never forget how you make them feel.

—PARKER J. PALMER

I have never reprimanded a boy in the evening—darkness and a troubled mind are a poor combination.

—FRANK L. BOYDEN

I have one rule—attention. They give me theirs and I give them mine.
—SISTER EVANGELIST, ON TEACHING HIGH SCHOOL STUDENTS, AS QUOTED IN *THE GAZETTE* (1980)

It takes time to persuade men to do even what is for their own good.
—THOMAS JEFFERSON, IN A LETTER TO REVEREND CHARLES CLAY (1790)

No trace of slavery ought to mix with the studies of the freeborn man . . . No study, pursued under compulsion, remains rooted in the memory.
—PLATO

Love is at the root of all healthy discipline.
—FRED ROGERS, FROM HIS BOOK *MISTER ROGERS TALKS WITH PARENTS* (1983)

Sometimes parents require new teachers to earn their trust. They view us as experimenting with their kid. If you show them you really care, then they are supportive.
—MIKE BENEVENTO, TEACHER FROM UPPER SADDLE RIVER, NEW JERSEY, AS QUOTED IN *SURVIVAL GUIDE FOR NEW TEACHERS* (2000)

We must accept finite disappointment, but we must never lose infinite hope.
—MARTIN LUTHER KING JR.

Strength does not come from physical capacity. It comes from an indomitable will.
—Mahatma Gandhi

Before you can inspire with emotion, you must be swamped with it yourself. Before you can move their tears, your own must flow. To convince them, you must yourself believe.
—Winston Churchill

Be kind whenever possible . . . It is always possible.
—Dalai Lama

There will be stumbling blocks or stepping stones; it all depends on how we use them.
—Anonymous

An atmosphere of trust, love, and humor can nourish extraordinary human capacity.
—MARILYN FERGUSON, FROM HER BOOK *THE AQUARIAN CONSPIRACY* (1987)

Children love repetition, but not when it's overdone. They will lose interest if you progress too slowly, and if you go too quickly the materials will be beyond their comprehension.
—ELIZABETH G. HAINSTOCK, FROM HER BOOK *TEACHING MONTESSORI IN THE HOME* (1968)

If people do not try very hard to understand what a child says, he may come to feel that most of the time there is not much point in saying anything.
—JOHN HOLT, FROM HIS BOOK *HOW CHILDREN LEARN* (1967)

One great Reason why many Children abandon themselves wholly to silly sports and trifle away all their time insipidly is because they have found their Curiosity baulk'd and their Enquiries neglected. But had they been treated with more Kindness and Respect and their Questions answered, as they should, to their Satisfaction, I doubt not but they would have taken more Pleasure in Learning and improving their Knowledge.

—JOHN LOCKE, FROM HIS BOOK *SOME THOUGHTS CONCERNING EDUCATION AND OF THE CONDUCT OF THE UNDERSTANDING* (1693)

Allow time for your child to complete each activity that she begins.
—TERRY MALLOY, FROM HIS BOOK *MONTESSORI AND YOUR CHILD: A PRIMER FOR PARENTS* (1974)

The lines which are set for him for his imitation in writing should not contain useless sentences, but such as convey some moral instruction. The remembrance of such admonitions will attend him to old age, and will be of use even for the formation of his character.
—QUINTILIAN

If a child is reading aloud to you and comes to a word she doesn't understand, don't immediately ask her to sound it out. Instead, say, "What makes sense here?" Then the child has to think about how that word fits in with what she's been reading.

—Masha Kabakow Rudman, University of Massachusetts educator, as quoted in "Improved Reading Begins at Home, Where a Child Can See How Reading Fits in with Other Activities," the New York Times (1992)

I like to have a thing suggested rather than told in full. When every detail is given, the mind rests satisfied and the imagination loses the desire to use its own wings.

—Thomas Bailey Aldrich

Be all that you can be. Find your future—as a teacher.

—Madeline Fuchs Holzer, Arts in Education director for the New York State Council on the Arts

I wish I could persuade every teacher to be proud of his occupation—not conceited or pompous, but proud. People who introduce themselves with the shame remark that they are, "just teachers," give me despair in my heart.

—William Garr

You can't direct the wind but you can adjust the sails.

—Anonymous

If you want to make good use of your time, you've got to know what's most important and then give it all you've got.

—Lee Iacocca, American industrialist and former head of Chrysler

You must first know what people need, and then invest yourself where you are most needed.

—Russell H. Conwell, American Baptist minister, lawyer, writer, orator, and founder of Temple University

I always prefer to believe the best of everybody; it saves so much trouble.

—Rudyard Kipling

Attitudes are more important than facts.

—Karl A. Menninger

One of the best ways to persuade others is with your ears—by listening to them.

—Dean Rusk, former U.S. Secretary of State

I can but think that the world would be better and brighter if our teachers would dwell on the duty of happiness as well as the happiness of duty; for we ought to be as bright and genial as we can, if only because to be cheerful ourselves is a most effectual contribution to the happiness of others.

—JOHN LUBBOCK

A compliment is verbal sunshine.

—ROBERT ORBEN, AMERICAN MAGICIAN AND COMEDY WRITER

The purpose of education is to make the choices clear to people, not to make the choices for people.

—PETER MCWILLIAMS, WRITER AND CANNABIS ACTIVIST

You need to be aware of what others are doing, applaud their efforts, acknowledge their successes, and encourage them in their pursuits. When we all help one another, everybody wins.

—JIM STOVALL

We must have the courage to examine everything, discuss everything, and even to teach everything.

—CONDORCET, MATHEMATICIAN AND EARLY POLITICAL SCIENTIST

All students can learn and succeed, but not in the same day, in the same way.

—WILLIAM G. SPADY

Education should be the process of helping everyone to discover his uniqueness, to teach him how to develop that uniqueness, and then to show him how to share it because that's the only reason for having anything.
—Dr. Leo Buscaglia

We should never pretend to know what we don't know, we should not feel ashamed to ask and learn from people below, and we should listen carefully to the views of the cadres at the lowest levels. Be a pupil before you become a teacher; learn from the cadres at the lower levels before you issue orders.
—Mao Tse-Tung

You teach a little by what you say. You teach the most by what you are.
—Henrietta Mears

Interest can produce learning on a scale compared to fear as a nuclear explosion to a firecracker.
—Stanley Kubrick

One of the great strengths of caring as an ethos is that it does not assume that all students should be treated by some impartial standards of fairness. Some students need more attention than others.
—Nel Noddings, from her book *Caring: A Feminist Perspective* (1984)

Do not appear so scholarly, I pray you.
Humanize your talk, and speak to be
understood. Do you think a Greek name
gives more weight to your reasons?

—MOLIÈRE

If you are truly serious about preparing
your child for the future, don't teach him to
subtract—teach him to deduct.

—FRAN LEBOWITZ, FROM HER BOOK SOCIAL STUDIES
(1981)

You cannot teach a man anything;
you can only help him find it within
himself.

—GALILEO GALILEI

Kind words can be short and easy to speak, but their echoes are endless.

—Mother Teresa

When discipline was required, I tried to dole it out in a manner that was firm but fair, with no emotionalism or anger attached. Anger prevents proper thinking and makes you vulnerable.

—John Wooden, from his book *My Personal Best* (2004)

Practice is the best of all instructors.

—Publilius Syrus

Children have real understanding only of that which they invent themselves, and each time that we try to teach them too quickly, we keep them from reinventing it themselves.
—JEAN PIAGET

Not many of you should become teachers, my brothers and sisters, for you know that we who teach will be judged with greater strictness.
—JAMES 3:1

Are we influencing student's self-concept in positive or negative ways? . . . How can a person feel liked unless somebody likes him? How can a person feel wanted unless somebody wants him? . . . And how can a person feel that he is capable unless he has some success?
—ARTHUR COMBS

It is no matter what you teach them first, any more than what leg you shall put into your breeches first. You may stand disputing which is best to put in first, but in the mean time your breech is bare.
—SAMUEL JOHNSON

The most prominent requisite to a lecturer, though perhaps not really the most important, is a good delivery; . . . I am sorry to say that the generality of mankind cannot accompany us one short hour unless the path is strewn with flowers.

—MICHAEL FARADAY, AS QUOTED IN *ADVICE TO A LECTURER* (1960)

There is no such whetstone, to sharpen a good wit and encourage a will to learning, as is praise.

—ROGER ASCHAM

A pupil from whom nothing is ever demanded which he cannot do, never does all he can.

—JOHN STUART MILL, FROM HIS 1873 AUTOBIOGRAPHY

Let people realize clearly that every time they threaten someone or humiliate or hurt unnecessarily or dominate or reject another human being, they become forces for the creation of psychopathology, even if these be small forces. Let them recognize that every man who is kind, helpful . . . and warm, is a psychotherapeutic force.

—ABRAHAM MASLOW

You can't wipe away tears with notebook paper.

—CHARLES SCHULTZ

Too much rigidity on the part of teachers should be followed by a brisk spirit of insubordination on the part of the taught.

—AGNES REPPLIER

When inspiration does not come to me, I go
half way to meet it.
—Sigmund Freud

He who wishes to teach us a truth should
not tell it to us, but simply suggest it with a
brief gesture, a gesture which starts an ideal
trajectory in the air along which we glide until
we find ourselves at the feet of the new truth.
—Jose Ortega y Gasset

It is easier for a teacher to command
than to teach.
—John Locke

Pick battles big enough to matter, small enough to win.

—Jonathan Kozol, non-fiction writer, educator, and activist, from his book *On Being a Teacher* (1994)

Perhaps the most important single cause of a person's success or failure educationally has to do with the question of what he believes about himself.

—Arthur Combs

In nature there are neither rewards nor punishments—there are consequences.

—Robert Green Ingersoll

What a teacher doesn't say is a telling part of what a student hears.
—MAURICE NATANSON

A leader knows what's best to do; a manager knows merely how best to do it.
—KENNETH ADELMAN

You cannot manage men into battle. You manage things; you lead people.
—GRACE MURRAY HOPPER, NAVAL OFFICER AND PIONEER IN COMPUTER PROGRAMMING

No person can be a great leader unless he takes genuine joy in the successes of those under him.
—W. A. NANCE

You get the best effort from others not by lighting a fire beneath them, but by building a fire within.

—BOB NELSON

The key to successful leadership today is influence, not authority.

—KENNETH BLANCHARD

The speed of the leader determines the rate of the pack.

—WAYNE LUKAS

Teachers who inspire realize there will always be rocks in the road ahead of us.

—ANONYMOUS

The man who follows a crowd will never be followed by a crowd.
—S. Donnell

I found out that if you are going to win games, you had better be ready to adapt.
—Scotty Bowman, hockey coach

There are 86,400 seconds in a day. It's up to you to decide what to do with them.
—Jim Valvano

Coaches have to watch for what they don't want to see and listen to what they don't want to hear.
—John Madden

The first task of a leader is to keep hope alive.
—JOE BATTEN

I don't know any other way to lead but by example.
—DON SHULA

Setting a goal is not the main thing. It is deciding how you will go about achieving it and staying with that plan.
—KNUTE ROCKNE

Leadership is a matter of having people look at you and gain confidence, seeing how you react. If you're in control, they're in control.
—PAT RILEY

I believe managing is like holding a dove in your hand. If you hold it too tightly you kill it, but if you hold it too loosely, you lose it.
—TOMMY LASORDA

I do not believe in the gifted. If the students have *ganas* [Spanish for desire], I can make them do it.
—JAIME ESCALANTE, MATH TEACHER AND BASIS FOR THE FILM *STAND AND DELIVER* (1988)

My philosophy of learning, like my blood type, is be positive. Keeping student attitudes positive is vital to their success in learning.
—DAVID PLEACHER

A "no" uttered from deepest conviction is better and greater than a "yes" merely uttered to please, or what is worse, to avoid trouble.
—MAHATMA GANDHI

You don't have to teach people to be human. You need to teach them how to stop being inhuman.
—ELDRIDGE CLEAVER

If those about him will talk to him often about the Stories he has read and hear him tell them, it will, besides other Advantages, add Encouragement and Delight to his Reading, when he find there is some Use and Pleasure in it.
—JOHN LOCKE, FROM HIS BOOK *SOME THOUGHTS CONCERNING EDUCATION AND OF THE CONDUCT OF THE UNDERSTANDING* (1693)

Look up and not down; look forward and not back; look out and not in; and lend a hand.
—E. E. HALE

Impatience never commanded success.
—EDWIN H. CHAPIN

What gives light must endure burning.
—VIKTOR FRANKL

You have to have confidence in your ability, and then be tough enough to follow through.
—ROSALYNN CARTER

You cannot have a learning organization without a shared vision . . . A shared vision provides a compass to keep learning on course when stress develops.

—Peter Senge, author of *The Dance of Change* (1999)

I am sure it is one's duty as a teacher to try to show boys that no opinions, no tastes, no emotions are worth much unless they are one's own. I suffered acutely as a boy from the lack of being shown this.

—A. C. Benson

The secret to productive goal setting is in establishing clearly defined goals, writing them down, and then focusing on them several times a day with words, pictures, and emotions as if we've already achieved them.

—Denis Waitley

The work can wait while you show the child the rainbow, but the rainbow won't wait while you do the work.

—Patricia Clafford

It is not so much what is poured into the student, but what is planted that really counts.

—Anonymous

The powers of students sometimes sink under too great severity in correction . . . while they fear everything, they cease to attempt anything.

—QUINTILIAN

Let the no! once pronounced, be as a brazen wall, against which when a child hath some few times exhausted his strength without making any impression, he will never attempt to overthrown again.

—JEAN JACQUES ROUSSEAU

You can't hold a man down without staying down with him.

—BOOKER T. WASHINGTON

A decline in the extrinsic payoff requires a compensating improvement in the intrinsic satisfaction of learning if students are to be motivated.
—Henry M. Levin

There is no such thing as a weird human being. It's just that some people require more understanding than others do.
—Tom Robbins, from his book *Another Roadside Attraction* (1971)

No act of kindness, no matter how small, is ever wasted.
—Aesop

Work 'em hard, play 'em hard, feed 'em up to the nines and send 'em to bed so tired that they are asleep before their heads are on the pillow.
—Frank L. Boyden, as quoted in *News Summaries* (1954)

Fun is a good thing, but only when it spoils nothing better.
—George Santayana, from his book *The Sense of Beauty* (1896)

Do not use compulsion, but let early education be rather a sort of amusement.
—Plato

Those acquirements crammed by force into the mind of children simply clog and stifle intelligence. In order that knowledge be properly digested, it must be swallowed with a good appetite.

—ANATOLE FRANCE

Accustom your children constantly to this; if a thing happened at one window and they, when relating it, say that it happened at another do not let it pass, but instantly check them; you do not know where deviation from truth will end.

—SAMUEL JOHNSON

Your child is mainly interested in the process of doing things; he is not very concerned with the end results.
—TERRY MALLOY, FROM HIS BOOK *MONTESSORI AND YOUR CHILD: A PRIMER FOR PARENTS* (1974)

Most teachers waste their time by asking questions which are intended to discover what a pupil does not know whereas the true art of questioning has for its purpose to discover what the pupil knows or is capable of knowing.
—ALBERT EINSTEIN

Develop a built-in bullshit detector.
—ERNEST HEMINGWAY

Praise, like gold and diamonds, owes its values only to its scarcity.
—Samuel Johnson

Do not on any account attempt to write on both sides of the paper at once.
—W. C. Stellar and R. J. Yeatman, from their book *1066 and All That* (1930)

Erect no artificial walls that might limit potential, stifle creativity, or shackle innovation.
—Mike Krzyzewski

To suggest is to create—to describe is to destroy.
—Robert Doisneau

188

Language is a living, kicking, growing, flitting, evolving reality, and the teacher should spontaneously reflect its vibrant and protean qualities.
—JOHN A. RASSIAS, AS QUOTED IN *QUOTE* (1974)

It is not every question that deserves an answer.
—PUBLIUS SYRUS

Ask a silly question and you'll get a silly answer.
—AMERICAN PROVERB

If you don't like the question that's asked, answer some other question.
—HOWARD BAKER

189

The simplest questions are the hardest to answer.

—Northrop Frye

A question not to be asked is a question not to be answered.

—Robert Southby, from his book *The Doctor* (1812)

No answer is also an answer.

—Danish proverb

There's no good answer to a stupid question.
—Russian proverb

Almost all important questions are important
precisely because they are not susceptible to
quantitative answer.
—Arthur Schlesinger, Jr.

We teach what we like to learn and the reason many people go into teaching is vicariously to re-experience the primary joy experienced the first time they learned something they loved.
—STEPHEN BROOKFIELD

You are rewarding a teacher poorly if you remain always a pupil.
—FRIEDRICH NIETZSCHE

Teachers open the door. You enter by yourself.
—CHINESE PROVERB

Learning is not a spectator sport.
—ANONYMOUS

A master can tell you what he expects of you. A teacher, though, awakens your own expectations.

—Patricia Neal

The greatest sign of success for a teacher . . . is to be able to say, "The children are now working as if I did not exist."

—Maria Montessori

The dream begins with a teacher who believes in you, who tugs and pushes and leads you to the next plateau, sometimes poking you with a sharp stick called "truth."

—Dan Rather

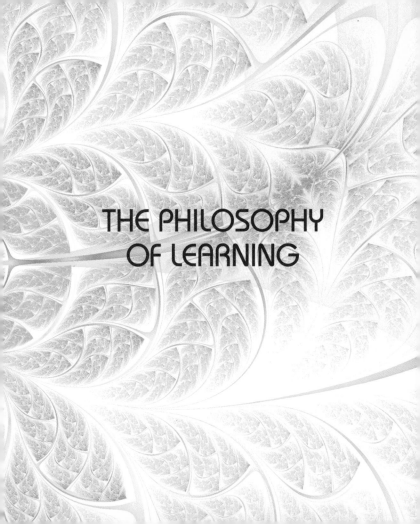

THE PHILOSOPHY
OF LEARNING

If I am walking with two other men, each of them will serve as my teacher. I will pick out the good points of the one and imitate them, and the bad points of the other and correct them in myself.

—CONFUCIUS

That is what learning is. You suddenly understand something you've understood all your life, but in a new way.

—DORIS LESSING

Learning to teach is a bigger job than universities, schools, experience, or personal disposition alone can accomplish.

—SHARON FEIMAN-NEMSER

Every student can learn, just not on the same day, or the same way.
—GEORGE EVANS

Learning without thought is labor lost; thought without learning is perilous.
—CONFUCIUS

You can teach a student a lesson for a day; but if you can teach him to learn by creating curiosity, he will continue the learning process as long as he lives.
—CLAY P. BEDFORD

Live as if you were to die tomorrow. Learn as if you were to live forever.
—GANDHI

I am learning all the time. The tombstone will be my diploma.

—EARTHA KITT

You learn something every day if you pay attention.

—RAY LEBLOND

I have never in my life learned anything from any man who agreed with me.

—DUDLEY FIELD MALONE

People learn something every day, and a lot of times it's that what they learned the day before was wrong.

—BILL VAUGHAN, FORMER COLUMNIST FOR THE *KANSAS CITY STAR*

The beautiful thing about learning is that no one can take it away from you.
—B.B. KING

The most useful piece of learning for the uses of life is to unlearn what is untrue.
—ANTISTHENES

Some people will never learn anything, for this reason, because they understand everything too soon.
—ALEXANDER POPE

Children have to be educated, but they have also to be left to educate themselves.
—ERNEST DIMNET, FROM HIS BOOK THE ART OF THINKING (1928)

A single conversation with a wise man is
better than ten years of study.
—CHINESE PROVERB

I don't think much of a man who is not wiser
today than he was yesterday.
—ABRAHAM LINCOLN

Beware of the man who works hard to
learn something, learns it, and finds
himself no wiser than before.
—KURT VONNEGUT

Learning is a treasure that will follow its
owner everywhere.
—CHINESE PROVERB

200

I am always ready to learn, although I do not always like being taught.
—Winston Churchill

There are many things which we can afford to forget which it is yet well to learn.
—Oliver Wendell Holmes, Jr.

I am defeated, and know it, if I meet any human being from whom I find myself unable to learn anything.
—George Herbert Palmer

I believe that the testing of the student's achievements in order to see if he meets some criterion held by the teacher, is directly contrary to the implications of therapy for significant learning.

—Carl Rogers

It's what you learn after you know it all that counts.

—Harry S. Truman

No matter how one may think himself accomplished, when he sets out to learn a new language, science, or the bicycle, he has entered a new realm as truly as if he were a child newly born into the world.

—Frances Willard, from her book *How I Learned to Ride the Bicycle*

Anyone who stops learning is old, whether at twenty or eighty. Anyone who keeps learning today is young. The greatest thing in life is to keep your mind young.
—HENRY FORD

It is not hard to learn more. What is hard is to unlearn when you discover yourself wrong.
—MARTIN H. FISCHER

You have learned something. That always feels at first as if you had lost something.
—H.G. WELLS (1866–1946)

Every act of conscious learning requires the willingness to suffer an injury to one's self-esteem. That is why young children, before they are aware of their own self-importance, learn so easily; and why older persons, especially if vain or important, cannot learn at all.

—THOMAS SZASZ, FROM HIS BOOK *THE SECOND SIN* (1973)

When there is much desire to learn, there of necessity will be much arguing, much writing, many opinions; for opinion in good men is but knowledge in the making.

—JOHN MILTON, FROM HIS BOOK *AREOPAGITICA* (1644)

It is through suffering that learning comes.

—AESCHYLUS

The justest division of human learning is that derived from the three different faculties of the soul, the seat of learning; history being relative to the memory, poetry to the imagination, and philosophy to the reason.

—FRANCIS BACON, FROM HIS BOOK *THE ADVANCEMENT OF LEARNING* (1605)

He that has less Learning than his Capacity is able to manage shall have more Use of it than he that has more than he can master. For no Man can have an active and ready Command of that which is too heavy for him.

—SAMUEL BUTLER, FROM "THOUGHTS ON VARIOUS SUBJECTS," *THE GENUINE REMAINS IN VERSE AND PROSE OF MR. SAMUEL BUTLER, AUTHOR OF HUDIBRAS* (1759)

Learning makes a man fit Company for himself.
—Thomas Fuller

A little learning misleadeth, and a great deal often stupifieth the understanding.
—Marquis of Halifax, from "False Learning," *Political, Moral and Miscellaneous Reflections* (1750)

And the same age saw Learning fall, and Rome.
—Alexander Pope, from his essay *An Essay on Criticism* (1711)

It is only when we forget all our learning that we begin to know.
—Henry David Thoreau, from his journal

Learning makes the wise wiser and the foolish more foolish.
—English proverb

Learning acquired in youth is inscribed on stone.
—Tamil proverb

We think too much about effective methods of teaching and not enough about effective methods of learning.
—John Carolus

Learning teacheth more in one year than experience in twenty, and learning teacheth safely, when experience maketh more miserable than wise . . . It is costly wisdom that is bought by experience.
—Roger Ascham

Learn from others what to pursue and what to avoid, and let your teachers be the lives of others.
—DIONYSIUS CATO

Learn one thing well first.
—JOHN CLARKE, IN *PROVERBS: ENGLISH AND LATINE* (1639)

In ancient times, men learned with a view to their own improvement. Nowadays, men learn with a view to the approbation of others.
—CONFUCIUS

A primary method of learning is to go from the familiar to the unfamiliar.

—GLENN DOMAN, FROM HIS BOOK *HOW TO TEACH YOUR BABY TO READ: THE GENTLE REVOLUTION* (1964)

What we have learned from others becomes our own by reflection.

—RALPH WALDO EMERSON, IN HIS "BLOTTING BOOK"

You are as who has a private door that leads him to the King's chamber. You have learned nothing rightly that you have not learned so.

—RALPH WALDO EMERSON, FROM HIS JOURNAL

It is impossible for a man to begin to learn what he thinks he knows.

—Epictetus, from *Discourses* (A.D. 101)

'Tis harder to unlearn than to learn.

—Thomas Fuller

You learn more from getting your butt kicked than from getting it kissed.

—Tom Hanks

Most learning is not the result of instruction. It is rather the result of unhampered participation in a meaningful setting.

—Ivan Illich, from his book, *Deschooling Society* (1970)

Learn to do good.

—Isaiah 1:17

Be done with rote learning And its attendant vexations.
—LAO-TZU

Robert F. Kennedy was one of the few adults, one of the few politicians, who kept learning after they grew up. Most of us just build up our intellectual capital and then live off it.
—FRANK MANKIEWICZ, FROM "OF KENNEDY AND KING," *SAN FRANCISCO SUNDAY EXAMINER & CHRONICLE*, JUNE 6, 1993

To learn is no easy matter and to apply what one has learned is even harder.
—MAO TSE-TUNG

Men are either learned or learning; the rest
are blockheads.

—MUHAMMAD

It is right to learn even from one's enemies.

—OVID

**Each day grow older, and learn
something new.**

—SOLON, ONE OF THE SEVEN SAGES OF GREECE

Let us learn on earth those things whose
knowledge might continue in heaven.

—ST. PAUL'S SCHOOL MOTTO, CONCORD, NEW
HAMPSHIRE

Before making a practical beginning on the job, the apprentice has had an opportunity to follow some general and summary course of instruction, so as to have a framework ready prepared in which to store the observations he is shortly to make. Furthermore he is able . . . to avail himself of sundry technical courses which he can follow in his leisure hours, so as to coordinate step by step the daily experience he is gathering.
—Hippolyte Adolphe Taine

Learn in order to teach and to practice.
—Talmud Rabbinical writings

Learn as though you would never be able to master it; hold it as though you would be in fear of losing it.
—CONFUCIUS

If you keep your mind sufficiently opened, people will throw a lot of rubbish into it.
—WILLIAM ORTON

I believe that children learn best when given the opportunity to taste, feel, see, hear, manipulate, discover, sing, and dance their way through learning.
—KATY GOLDMAN, TEACHER FROM PINE, ARIZONA, AS QUOTED IN *SURVIVAL GUIDE FOR NEW TEACHERS* (2002)

Only the curious will learn and only the resolute overcome the obstacles of learning. The quest quotient has always excited me more than the intelligence quotient.
—Eugene S. Wilson, as quoted in the *Reader's Digest* (1968)

I was taught the way of progress is neither swift nor easy.
—Marie Curie

The essence of learning is the ability to manage change by changing yourself.
—Arie de Gues, from his book *The Living Company* (1997)

Even without success, creative persons find joy in a job well done. Learning for its own sake is rewarding.

—MIHALY CSIKSZENTMIHALYI, FROM HIS BOOK *CREATIVITY: FLOW AND THE PSYCHOLOGY OF DISCOVERY AND INVENTION* (1997)

Creative activity could be described as a type of learning process where teacher and pupil are located in the same individual.

—ARTHUR KOESTLER

Learning is a social process that occurs through interpersonal interaction within a cooperative context. Individuals, working together, construct shared understandings and knowledge.

—David Johnson, from his book *Active Learning: Cooperation in the College Classroom* (1991)

Learning is often spoken of as if we were watching the open pages of all the books which we have ever read, and then, when occasion arises, we select the right page to read aloud to the universe.

—Alfred North Whitehead, as quoted in *The Teacher and the Taught* (1963)

Mistakes are the portals of discovery.
—JAMES JOYCE, FROM HIS BOOK *DUBLINERS*
(1914)

It is what we think we know already that often prevents us from learning.
—CLAUDE BERNARD

We learn well and fast when we experience the consequences of what we do—and don't do.
—ANONYMOUS

I find that a great part of the information I have was acquired by looking up something and finding something else on the way.
—FRANKLIN P. ADAMS

218

For many, learning is a spiral, where important themes are visited again and again throughout life, each time at a deeper, more penetrating level.
—JEROLD W. APS, FROM HIS BOOK *TEACHING FROM THE HEART* (1996)

One must learn by doing the thing, for though you think you know it, you have no certainty until you try.
—ARISTOTLE

Anxiety checks learning. An overall feeling of inferiority, a temporary humiliation, a fit of depression, defiance or anger, a sense of being rejected, and many other emotional disturbances affect the learning process. The reverse is true; a feeling of well-being and of being respected by others stimulates an alert mind, willingness to participate, and an attitude conducive to learning.

—EDNA LESHAN, FROM HER BOOK *THE CONSPIRACY AGAINST CHILDHOOD* (1967)

In the broadest sense, learning can be defined as a process of progressive change from ignorance to knowledge, from inability to competence, and from indifference to understanding.

—CAMERON FINCHER

Learning proceeds in fits and starts.
—Jerold W. Aps, from his book *Teaching from the Heart* (1996)

Learning is always rebellion . . . Every bit of new truth discovered is revolutionary to what was believed before.
—Margaret Lee Runbeck

Most people would say that what I am doing is "learning to play" the cello. But these words carry into our minds the strange idea that there exists two very different processes: One, learning to play the cello; and two, playing the cello . . . We learn to do something by doing it. There is no other way.
—John Holt

That's what learning is, after all; not whether we lose the game, but how we lose and how we've changed because to it and what we take away from it that we never had before.

—RICHARD BACH, IN HIS BOOK *THE BRIDGE ACROSS FOREVER* (1984)

I am still learning.

—MICHELANGELO

Learning is an active process. We learn by doing . . . Only knowledge that is used sticks in your mind.

—DALE CARNEGIE

You must learn day by day, year by year, to broaden your horizon. The more things you love, the more you are interested in, the more you enjoy, the more you are indignant about, the more you have left when anything happens.

—ETHEL BARRYMORE

Learning is a process of preparing to deal with new situations.

—ALVIN TOFFLER

Learning is discovering that something is possible.

—FRITZ PERLS

Whatever is good to know is difficult to learn.
—GREEK PROVERB

One of the weaknesses of our society is that history is still news to most people.
—GRANT FAIRLEY

Learn avidly. Question repeatedly what you have learned. Analyze it carefully. Then put what you have learned into practice intelligently.
—CONFUCIUS

Seeing much, suffering much, and studying much are the three pillars of learning.
—BENJAMIN DISRAELI

The moment you stop learning, you stop leading.
—Rick Warren

Learning is finding out what you already know, Doing is demonstrating that you know it, Teaching is reminding others that they know it as well as you do. We are all learners, doers, and teachers.
—Richard Bach

Learn as much as you can while you are young, since life becomes too busy later.
—Dana Stewart Scott

We learn more by looking for the answer to a question and not finding it than we do from learning the answer itself.
—LLOYD ALEXANDER

Learning is like rowing upstream: not to advance is to drop back.
—CHINESE PROVERB

We learn simply by the exposure of living, and what we learn most natively is the tradition in which we live.
—DAVID P. GARDNER

Nothing we learn in this world is ever wasted.
—ELEANOR ROOSEVELT

You don't understand anything until you learn it more than one way.
—Marvin Minsky

To learn, you must want to be taught.
—Proverbs 12:1

Wealth, if you use it, comes to an end; learning, if you can use it, increases.
—Swahili proverb

What we learn with pleasure we never forget.
—Louis Mercier

As long as you live, keep learning how to live.
—Lucius A. Seneca

Try to learn about everything and everything about something.

—Thomas Huxley

The illiterate of the twenty-first century will not be those who cannot read and write, but those who cannot learn, unlearn, and relearn.

—Alvin Toffler

The man who is too old to learn was probably always too old to learn.

—Henry S. Haskins

Learning is what most adults will do for a living in the twenty-first century.

—Bob Perelman

Never stop learning; knowledge doubles every fourteen months.

—Anthony J. D'Angelo, from his book *The College Blue Book* (1995)

I have never met a man so ignorant that I couldn't learn something from him.

—Galileo Galilei

Learning is not compulsory . . . neither is survival.

—W. Edwards Deming

Learning is not attained by chance. It must be sought for with ardor and attended to with diligence.

—Abigail Adams

All learning begins with the simple phrase, "I don't know."
—ANONYMOUS

Of all the civil rights for which the world has struggled and fought for 5,000 years, the right to learn is undoubtedly the most fundamental.
—W. E. B. DuBois

When asked what learning was the most necessary, he said, "Not to unlearn what you have learned!"
—DIOGENES LAERTIUS, BIOGRAPHER OF ANCIENT GREEK PHILOSOPHERS

Learning is never done without errors and defeat.
—Vladimir Lenin

He is educated who knows where to find out what he doesn't know.
—Georg Simmel

Try to put into practice what you already know, and in doing so you will in good time discover the hidden things which you now inquire about.
—Henry Van Dyke

If a man will begin with certainties, he shall end in doubts; but if he will be content to begin with doubts, he shall end in certainties.

—Francis Bacon, from his book *The Advancement of Learning* (1605)

In completing one discovery we never fail to get an imperfect knowledge of others of which we could have no idea before, so that we cannot solve one doubt without creating several new ones.

—Joseph Priestly

Much that passes for education . . . is not education at all but ritual. The fact is that we are being educated when we know it least.

—David P. Gardner

It is by extending oneself, by exercising some capacity previously unused, that you come to a better knowledge of your own potential.

—HAROLD BLOOM, IN *SHORT STORIES AND POEMS FOR EXCEPTIONALLY INTELLIGENT CHILDREN* (2001)

I don't divide the world into the weak and the strong, or the successes and the failures, those who make it or those who don't. I divide the world into learners and non-learners.

—BENJAMIN BARBER

If you study to remember, you will forget, but if you study to understand, you will remember.

—ANONYMOUS

No matter how occupied a man may be, he must snatch at least one hour for study daily.

—THE BRATZLAVER, IN LOUIS I. NEWMAN'S COMPOSITION, *THE HASIDIC ANTHOLOGY* (1934)

The elevation of the mind ought to be the principal end of all our studies.

—EDMUND BURKE, IN HIS BOOK *A PHILOSOPHICAL INQUIRY INTO THE ORIGIN OF OUR IDEAS OF THE SUBLIME AND THE BEAUTIFUL* (1756)

Let the great book of the world be your principal study.

—LORD CHESTERFIELD, IN A LETTER TO HIS SON (1751)

Study the teachings of the Great Sages of all sects impartially.

—GAMPOPA, TIBETAN RELIGIOUS LEADER

234

The love of study, a passion which derives fresh vigor from enjoyment, supplies each day, each hour, with a perpetual source of independent and rational pleasure.

—EDWARD GIBBON, IN HIS BOOK *MEMOIRS OF MY LIFE AND WRITINGS* (1869)

Alexander Pope, finding little advantage from external help, resolved thenceforward to direct himself, and at twelve formed a plan of study which he completed with little other incitement than the desire of excellence.

—SAMUEL JOHNSON, FROM "POPE," *LIVES OF ENGLISH POETS* (1781)

Just as eating contrary to the inclination is injurious to the health, so study without desire spoils the memory, and it retains nothing that it takes in.
—Leonardo da Vinci

Study in joy and good cheer, in accordance with your intelligence and heart's dictates.
—Rashi

The great business of study is to form a mind adapted and adequate to all times and all occasions; to which all nature is then laid open, and which may be said to possess the key of her inexhaustible riches.
—Sir Joshua Reynolds, from "Discourse Eleven," *Discourses on Art* (1769–1790)

I don't love studying. I hate studying. I like learning. Learning is beautiful.
—Natalie Portman

The man who graduates today and stops learning tomorrow is uneducated the day after.
—Newton D. Baker

Every successful learning initiative requires key people to allocate hours to new types of activities: reflection, planning, collaborative work, and training.
—Peter Senge, from his book *The Dance of Change* (1999)

If you can't learn to do it well, learn to enjoy doing it badly.
—ASHLEIGH BRILLIANT, ENGLISH AUTHOR AND SYNDICATED CARTOONIST

The classroom, not the trench, is the frontier of freedom now and forevermore.
—LYNDON B. JOHNSON

Restraint and discipline and examples of virtue and justice. These are the things that form the education of the world.
—EDMUND BURKE

To say "well done" to any bit of good work is to take hold of the powers which have made the effort and strengthen them beyond our knowledge.
—PHILLIPS BROOKS

Results are better than intentions.
—Dr. Phil McGraw

It was an initiation into the love of learning,
of learning how to learn, that was revealed
to me by my BLS masters as a matter of
interdisciplinary cognition—that is, learning
to know something by its relation to something
else.
—Leonard Bernstein, on the Boston Latin School, as
quoted in the *New York Times* (1984)

A little learning is a dangerous thing;
drink of it deeply, or taste it not, for
shallow thoughts intoxicate the brain,
and drinking deeply sobers us again.
—Alexander Pope

They know enough who know how to learn.
—Henry Adams

To every answer you can find a new question.
—Yiddish proverb

The very fact of its finding itself in agreement with other minds perturbs it, so that it hunts for points of divergence, feeling the urgent need to make it clear that at least it reached the same conclusions by a different route.
—Sir Herbert Butterfield, in his 1961 retirement address

He who is ashamed of asking is ashamed of learning.

—Danish proverb

The artificial method of learning is to hear what other people say, to learn and to read, and so to get your head crammed full of general ideas before you have any sort of extended acquaintance with the world as it is, and as you may see it for yourself.

—Arthur Schopenhauer, from "On Education," Studies in Pessimism (1851)

We cannot seek or attain health, wealth, learning, justice, or kindness in general. Action is always specific, concrete, individualized, unique.

—Benjamin Jowett

Much learning does not teach
understanding.
—HERACLITUS

If you employed study, thinking, and planning
time daily, you could develop and use the
power that can change the course of your
destiny.
—W. CLEMENT STONE

Whether one has natural talent or
not, any learning period requires the
willingness to suffer uncertainty and
embarrassment.
—GAIL SHEEHY

Let us rise up and be thankful, for if we didn't learn a lot today, at least we learned a little, and if we didn't learn a little, at least we didn't get sick, and if we got sick, at least we didn't die; so let us all be thankful.
—BUDDHA

The brighter you are, the more you have to learn.
—DON HEROLD

Creativity is a type of learning process where the teacher and pupil are located in the same individual.
—ARTHUR KOESTLER

Apply yourself. Get all the education you can, but then, by God, do something. Don't just stand there; make it happen.

—LEE IACOCCA

There is divine beauty in learning, just as there is human beauty in tolerance. To learn means to accept the postulate that life did not begin at my birth. Others have been here before me, and I walk in their footsteps.

—ELIE WIESEL

Nature without learning is blind, learning apart from nature is fractional, and practice in the absence of both is aimless.

—PLUTARCH

He not only overflowed with learning, but stood in the slop.
—SYDNEY MITH OF MACAULAY

I learned to make my mind large, as the universe is large, so that there is room for paradoxes.
—MAXINE HONG KINGSTON

I will study and get ready and someday my chance will come.
—ABRAHAM LINCOLN

If you stuff yourself full of poems, essays, plays, stories, novels, films, comic strips, magazines, music, you automatically explode every morning like old faithful. I have never had a dry spell in my life, mainly because I feed myself well, to the point of bursting. I wake early and hear my morning voices leaping around in my head like jumping beans. I get out of bed to trap them before they escape.

—RAY BRADBURY

That which we obtain too easily, we esteem too lightly.

—THOMAS PAINE

I do not pray for a lighter load, but for a stronger back.
—Phillips Brooks

In times of change, learners inherit the earth; while the learned find themselves beautifully equipped to deal with a world that no longer exists.
—Eric Hoffer

The only person who is educated is the one who has learned how to learn and change.
—Carl Rogers

Whoever neglects learning in his youth, loses the past and is dead to the future.
—Euripides

We do not learn by inference and deduction and the application of mathematics to philosophy, but by direct intercourse and sympathy.

—Henry David Thoreau, from his book *Natural History of Massachusetts* (1842)

At present there are differences of opinion . . . for all people do not agree as to the things that the young ought to learn, either with a view to virtue or with a view to the best life, nor is it clear whether their studies should be regulated more with regard to intellect or with regard to character.

—Aristotle

In all the things we learn only from those whom we love.
—Johann Wolfgang von Goethe

It is my firm conviction that a man can learn more about poetry by really knowing and examining a few of the best poems than by meandering about among a great many.
—Ezra Pound, from his book *ABC of Reading* (1934)

Develop a passion for learning. If you do, you will never cease to grow.
—Anthony J. D'Angelo, from his book *The College Blue Book* (1995)

Study to be quiet.
—Izaak Walton, from his book *The Complete Angler* (1653)

If you rest, you rust.
—HELEN HAYES, FROM HER BOOK *MY LIFE IN THREE ACTS* (1990)

I know of no more encouraging fact than the unquestionable ability of man to elevate his life by conscious endeavor.
—HENRY DAVID THOREAU

The proper study of mankind is man.
—ALEXANDER POPE

All men who have turned out worth anything have had the chief hand in their own education.
—SIR WALTER SCOTT

No one can become really educated without having pursued some study in which he took no interest.

—T.S. Eliot

The beginning is the most important part of the work.

—Plato

Gie me ae spark o' Nature's fire. That's a' the learning I desire.

—Robert Burns, from "Epistle to J. Lapraik," *Poems, Mainly in the Scottish Dialect* (1786)

The best learners . . . often make the worst teachers. They are, in a very real sense, perceptually challenged. They cannot imagine what it must be like to struggle to learn something that comes so naturally to them.
—STEPHEN BROOKFIELD

To make headway, improve your head.
—B. C. FORBES

The same man cannot be skilled in everything, each has his own special excellence.
—EURIPIDES

Everyone is ignorant, only on different subjects.
—WILL ROGERS

It iz better tew know nothing than two know what ain't so.
—John Billings, from "Sollum Thoughts," *Everybody's Friend* (1874)

Opposites are not contradictory but complementary.
—Niels Bohr

I had also started studying because I wanted to learn more about power and fighting.
—Lou Reed

We must learn our limits. We are all something, but none of us are everything.
—Blaise Pascal

253

Get over the idea that only children should spend their time in study. Be a student so long as you still have something to learn, and this will mean all your life.

—Henry L. Doherty

Simply making consistent investments in our self-education and knowledge banks pays major dividends throughout our lives.

—Jim Rohn, motivational coach

What a relief it was to discover that I wasn't really an idiot! I simply had a learning disability.

—John H. Johnson founder of the largest African American publishing company in America, Johnson Publishing Company

Poor is the pupil who does not surpass his master.
—LEONARDO DA VINCI

There is no subject so old that some-thing new cannot be said about it.
—FYODOR DOSTOEVSKY

Cultivate the habit of attention and try to gain opportunities to hear wise men and women talk. Indifference and inattention are the two most dangerous monsters that you ever meet. Interest and attention will insure to you an education.
—ROBERT A. MILLIKAN

It is important that students bring a certain ragamuffin, barefoot irreverence to their studies; they are not here to worship what is known, but to question it.

—Jacob Bronowski

Learned men are the cisterns of knowledge, not the fountainheads.

—James Northcote

Better is the enemy of good.
—Voltaire

There is always room at the top.

—Daniel Webster

Lack of something to feel important about is almost the greatest tragedy a man may have.

—ARTHUR E. MORGAN

The barriers are not erected which can say to aspiring talents and industry, "Thus far and no farther."

—LUDWIG VAN BEETHOVEN

Nothing would be done, at all, if we waited until we could do it so well that no one could find fault with it.

—JOHN HENRY CARDINAL NEWMAN

Education: n., the process of nourishing or rearing.
—*The Shorter Oxford English Dictionary*

One's work may be finished some day, but one's education never.
—*Alexander Dumas*

Education is man's going forward from cocksure ignorance to thoughtful uncertainty.
—*Kenneth G. Johnson*

The task of education is to make the individual so firm and sure that, as a whole being, he can no longer be diverted from his path.
—*Friedrich Nietzsche from his book Human, All Too Human* (1878)

Education is bitter but the fruit is sweet.
—Agustin Marissa

Education is light, lack of it darkness.
—Russian proverb

Your Education is worth what You are worth.
—Anonymous

The educated differ from the uneducated as much as the living from the dead.
—Aristotle

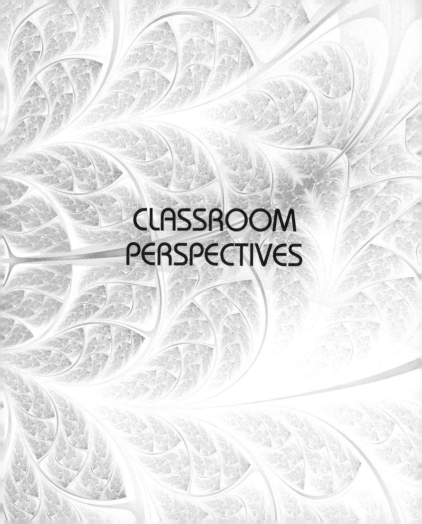

CLASSROOM
PERSPECTIVES

Real education must ultimately be limited to men who insist on knowing—the rest is mere sheep-herding.

—EZRA POUND

Education is a specifically human activity. Unlike other animals, man inherits something over and above what is transmitted to him automatically by physical and psychic heredity.

—ARNOLD J. TOYNBEE, AS QUOTED IN *THE TEACHER AND THE TAUGHT* (1963)

Education: Being able to differentiate between what you do know and what you don't. It's knowing where to go to find out what you need to know; and it's knowing how to use the information once you get it.

—WILLIAM FEATHER

Education is the point at which we decide whether we love the world enough to assume responsibility for it.

—HANNAH ARENDT

263

Real education should educate us out of self into something far finer; into a selflessness which links us with all humanity.

—NANCY ASTOR, THE FIRST WOMAN TO SERVE AS A MEMBER OF THE BRITISH HOUSE OF COMMONS

Education is the power to think clearly, the power to act well in the world's work, and the power to appreciate life.

—BRIGHAM YOUNG

Education is an ornament in prosperity and a refuge in adversity.

—ARISTOTLE

We need education in the obvious more than investigation of the obscure.
—Oliver Wendell Holmes, Jr., in a speech at a dinner of the Harvard Law School Association of New York, 1913

An education isn't how much you have committed to memory, or even how much you know. It's being able to differentiate between what you know and what you don't.
—Malcolm S. Forbes

To repeat what others have said, requires education; to challenge it, requires brains.
—Mary Pettibone Poole

An educated man is one who can entertain a new idea, entertain another person, and entertain himself.
—SYDNEY WOOD

The very spring and root of honesty and virtue lie in good education.
—PLUTARCH

Education is the art of making man ethical.
—GEORG HEGEL, IN HIS BOOK *THE PHILOSOPHY OF RIGHT* (1821)

Intelligence plus character—that is the goal of true education.
—MARTIN LUTHER KING, JR.

All genuine education is liberating, and certainly needs freedom and discipline.
—REGINALD D. ARCHAMBAULT, FROM HIS BOOK *JOHN DEWEY ON EDUCATION* (1964)

The quality of strength lined with tenderness is an unbeatable combination, as are intelligence and necessity when unblunted by formal education.
—MAYA ANGELOU

True education makes for inequality; the inequality of individuality, the inequality of success, the glorious inequality of talent, of genius.
—FELIX E. SCHELLING, AMERICAN EDUCATOR

The principle goal of education is to create men who are capable of doing new things, not simply of repeating what other generations have done—men who are creative, inventive and discoverers.

—JEAN PIAGET

Education makes people easy to lead, but difficult to drive; easy to govern, but impossible to enslave.

—HENRY PETER BROUGHAN

The highest result of education is tolerance.

—HELEN KELLER

It is very nearly impossible . . . to become an educated person in a country so distrustful of the independent mind.
—James Baldwin

If you say you understand something, then you can explain what you understand to others. Anything short of that is deception, not understanding. Education, above all, should not be about fostering deception.
—R.J. Kizlik

Education is a method whereby one acquires a higher grade of prejudices.
—Laurence J. Peter

Education is the process of driving a set of prejudices down your throat.
—Martin H. Fischer

Next in importance to freedom and justice is popular education, without which neither freedom nor justice can be permanently maintained.
—James A. Garfield

Only the educated are free.
—Epictetus

The whole purpose of education is to turn mirrors into windows.
—Sydney J. Harris

Education is simply the soul of a society as it passes from one generation to another.
—G.K. CHESTERTON

I read Shakespeare and the Bible and I can shoot dice. That's what I call a liberal education.
—TALLULAH BANKHEAD

The primary purpose of a liberal education is to make one's mind a pleasant place in which to spend one's time.
—SYDNEY J. HARRIS

The liberally educated person is one who is able to resist the easy and preferred answers not because he is obstinate but because he knows others worthy of consideration.

—ALLAN BLOOM

The gains in education are never really lost. Books may be burned and cities sacked, but truth, like the yearning for freedom, lives in the hearts of humble men.

—FRANKLIN DELANO ROOSEVELT

Formal education is but an incident in the lifetime of an individual. Most of us who have given the subject any study have come to realize that education is a continuous process ending only when ambition comes to a halt.

—R. I. REES

Vitally important for a young man or woman is, first, to realize the value of education and then to cultivate earnestly, aggressively, ceaselessly, the habit of self-education.

—B. C. FORBES

An educational system isn't worth a great deal if it teaches young people how to make a living but doesn't teach them how to make a life.

—ANONYMOUS

Education is the drawing out of the soul.

—RALPH WALDO EMERSON

Education is the manifestation of the perfection already in man.

—SWAMI VIVEKANANDA

The great secret of education is to make the exercises of the body and the mind serve as relaxation to each other.

—JEAN JACQUES ROUSSEAU

The most important outcome of education is to help students become independent of formal education.
—PAUL E. GRAY, PRESIDENT OF THE MASSACHUSETTS INSTITUTE OF TECHNOLOGY

A wise system of education will at last teach us how little man yet knows, how much he has still to learn.
—SIR JOHN LUBBOCK

Without education, you're not going anywhere in this world.
—MALCOLM X

Education is not preparation for life; education is life itself.
—JOHN DEWEY

Invest in yourself, in your education. There's nothing better.
—Sylvia Porter

Education is one of the few things a person is willing to pay for and not get.
—William Lowe Bryan

A good education is like a savings account; the more you put into it, the richer you are.
—Anonymous

Education costs money, but then so does ignorance.
—Sir Claude Moser

Genius without education is like silver in the mine.

—Benjamin Franklin

Formal education will make you a living; self-education will make you a fortune.

—Jim Rohn, motivational coach

If you think education is expensive, try ignorance.

—Derek Bok, from his book *Universities and the Future of America* (1990)

The day someone quits school he is condemning himself to a future of poverty.

—Jaime Escalante, math teacher and basis for the film *Stand and Deliver* (1988)

The great aim of education is not knowledge but action.
—Herbert Spencer

Information cannot replace education.
—Earl Kiole

An educated person is one who has learned that information almost always turns out to be at best incomplete and very often false, misleading, fictitious, mendacious—just dead wrong.
—Russell Baker

Education is not the answer to the question. Education is the means to the answer to all questions.
—William Allin

278

Schooling, instead of encouraging
the asking of questions, too often
discourages it.
—MADELEINE L'ENGLE

The one real goal of education is to leave a
person asking questions.
—MAX BEERBOHM

The one real object of education is
to have a man in the condition of
continually asking questions.
—BISHOP MANDELL CREIGHTON

It is the mark of an educated mind to be able
to entertain a thought without accepting it.
—ARISTOTLE

279

One of the greatest problems of our time is that many are schooled but few are educated.
—THOMAS MOORE

Education is that which discloses to the wise and disguises from the foolish their lack of understanding.
—AMBROSE BIERCE

Education consists mainly of what we have unlearned.
—MARK TWAIN

Much that passes for education is not education at all but ritual. The fact is that we are being educated when we know it least.
—DAVID P. GARDNER

Education is the ability to listen to almost anything without losing your temper.
—Robert Frost

One of the benefits of a college education is to show the boy its little avail.
— Ralph Waldo Emerson

The very spring and root of honesty and virtue lie in good education.
—Titus Vespasianus

Education, properly understood, is that which teaches discernment.
—Joseph Roux

There is only one curriculum, no matter what the method of education: what is basic and universal in human experience and practice, the underlying structure of culture.
—PAUL GOODMAN

Upon the subject of education, not presuming to dictate any plan or system respecting it, I can only say that I view it as the most important subject which we as a people may be engaged in.
— ABRAHAM LINCOLN

The best education consists in immunizing people against systematic attempts at education.
—PAUL KARL FEYERABEND

They teach in academies far too many things, and far too much that is useless.
—Johann Wolfgang Von Goethe

Education is like a double-edged sword. It may be turned to dangerous uses if it is not properly handled.
—Wu Ting-Fang

Education can be dangerous. It is very difficult to make it not dangerous. In fact, it is almost impossible.
—Robert M. Hutchins

Education would be so much more effective if its purpose were to ensure that by the time they leave school every boy and girl should know how much they don't know, and be imbued with a lifelong desire to know it.

—Sir William Haley

Education is the period during which you are being instructed by somebody you do not know, about something you do not want to know.

—Gilbert K. Chesterton

The well-meaning people who talk about education as if it were a substance distributable by coupon in large or small quantities never exhibit any understanding of the truth that you cannot teach anybody anything that he does not want to learn.
—GEORGE SAMPSON

Education is our passport to the future, for tomorrow belongs to the people who prepare for it today.
—MALCOLM X

I am convinced that it is of primordial importance to learn more every year than the year before. After all, what is education but a process by which a person begins to learn how to learn?
—PETER USTINOV

Education is the ability to meet life's situations.
—DR. JOHN G. HIBBEN, FORMER PRESIDENT OF PRINCETON UNIVERSITY

The best educated human being is the one who understands most about the life in which he is placed.
—HELEN KELLER

Let us think of education as the means of developing our greatest abilities, because in each of us there is a private hope and dream which, fulfilled, can be translated into benefit for everyone and greater strength for our nation.
—John F. Kennedy

The education of a man is never completed until he dies.
—Robert E. Lee

A final reason for making education a process of self-instruction, and by consequence a process of pleasurable instruction, we may advert to the fact that, in proportion as it is made so, is here a probability that it will not cease when school days end.

—Herbert Spencer

Education is the best provision for old age.

—Aristotle

No man who worships education has got the best out of education . . . Without a gentle contempt for education, no man's education is complete.

—G.K. Chesterton

Education, like neurosis, begins at home.
—Milton Sapirstein

You speak of beginning the education of your son. The moment he was able to form an idea his education was already begun.
—Anna Laetitia Barbauld

What the child says, he has heard at home.
—African proverb

Who takes the child by the hand takes the mother by the heart.
—German proverb

One mother can achieve more than a hundred teachers.
—JEWISH PROVERB

The family fireside is the best of schools.
—ARNOLD H. GLASOW

I doubt that we can ever successfully impose values or attitudes or behaviors on our children—certainly not by threat, guilt, or punishment. But I do believe they can be induced through relationships where parents and children are growing together. Such relationships are, I believe, built on trust, example, talk, and caring.
—FRED ROGERS

290

My grandmother wanted me to have an education, so she kept me out of school.
—MARGARET MEAD

The group consisting of mother, father, and child is the main educational agency of mankind.
—MARTIN LUTHER KING, JR.

School is an invaluable adjunct to the home, but it is a wretched substitute for it.
—THEODORE ROOSEVELT

Parents must acknowledge that the schooling which will be best for their children in the twenty-first century must be very different from the schooling they experienced themselves.

—Andy Hargreaves and Michael Fullan, from their book *What's Worth Fighting for Out There?* (1998)

Showing up at school already able to read is like showing up at the undertaker's already embalmed: people start worrying about being put out of their jobs.

—Florence King

They say that we are better educated than our parents' generation. What they mean is that we go to school longer. It is not the same thing.
—RICHARD YATES

There are three important qualities of a good family. These are love, cooperation, and positive expectations. So it should be in a good school.
—WILLIAM COOPER SMITH

Education begins at home. You can't blame the school for not putting into your child what you don't put into him.
—GEOFFREY HOLDER

293

Examinations are formidable even to the best prepared, for the greatest fool may ask more than the wisest man can answer.

—CHARLES CALEB COLTON

Trying to teach children without involving parents is like raking leaves in high wind.

—DR. KIMBERLY MUHAMMAD-EARL

This is the great vice of academicism, that it is concerned with ideas rather than with thinking.

—LIONEL TRILLING

It has been said that the primary function of schools is to impart enough facts to make children stop asking questions. Some, with whom the schools do not succeed, become scientists.

—Knut Schmidt-Nielsen

Education is what happens to the other person, not what comes out of the mouth of the educator.

—Miles Horton

Much education today is monumentally ineffective. All too often we are giving young people cut flowers when we should be teaching them to grow their own plants.

—John W. Gardner

Teachers should be able to teach subjects, not manuals merely.
—HORACE MANN, AS QUOTED BY LAWRENCE A. CREMIN IN *THE REPUBLIC AND THE SCHOOL* (1957)

Education is not the piling of learning, information, data, facts, skills, or abilities—that's training or instruction—but is rather a making visible what is hidden as a seed.
—THOMAS MOORE

Ideas, facts, relationships, stories, histories, possibilities, artistry in words, in sounds, in form and in color, crowd into the child's life, stir his feelings, excite his appreciation, and incite his impulses to kindred activities. It is a saddening thought that on this golden age there falls so often the shadow of the crammer.

—ALFRED NORTH WHITEHEAD, AS QUOTED IN *THE TEACHER AND THE TAUGHT* (1963)

Education is not something which the teacher does . . . it is a natural process which develops spontaneously in the human being.

—MARIA MONTESSORI

All genuine learning is active, not passive. It involves the use of the mind, not just the memory. It is a process of discovery, in which the student is the main agent, not the teacher.

—Mortimer J. Adler

The modern child, when asked what he learned today, replies, "Nothing, but I gained some meaningful insights.

—Bill Vaughan, in *The Paideia Proposal: An Educational Manifesto* (1982)

The most effective kind of education is that a child should play amongst lovely things.

—Plato

Phonetics, word associations, sentence structure, and all the techniques of good reading must be taught and drilled, but do not let us confuse these with reading. As teachers, let us learn how to prepare our reading lessons so that they serve to stir and strengthen the wings of imagination which may help our children to read the reality of life when they enter it as adult human beings.

—HENRY BARNES

All of us learn to write in the second grade. Most of us go on to greater things.

—BOBBY KNIGHT

Parochial schools gave me a good early education. They made it possible for me to begin writing stories and even one novel at the age of eleven.
—Jack Kerouac

The chief reason for going to school is to get the impression fixed for life that there is a book side for everything.
—Robert Frost

The objective of education is to prepare the young to educate themselves throughout their lives.
—Robert Maynard Hutchins

Education: What remains after you have forgotten all that you have been taught.
—LORD HALIFAX, ARISTOCRAT, POLITICIAN, AND WAR SECRETARY OF BRITAIN DURING WWII

The function of education is to help you from childhood not to imitate anybody, but be yourself all the time.
—JIDDU KRISHNAMURTI

The aim of education should be to teach us rather how to think, than what to think—rather to improve our minds, so as to enable us to think for ourselves, than to load the memory with the thoughts of other men.
—BILL BEATTIE

Education must not simply teach work—it must teach life.
—W. E. B. DuBois

Education does not mean teaching people to know what they do not know; it means teaching them to behave as they do not behave.
—John Ruskin

Education must have an end in view, for it is not an end in itself.
—Sybil Marshall

It will be a great day when our schools get all the money they need and the Air Force has to hold a bake sale to buy a bomber.
—Anonymous

302

It is not in the power of one generation to form a complete plan of education.
—IMMANUEL KANT, AS QUOTED IN *THE TEACHER AND THE TAUGHT* (1963)

Uniting a school behind an academic endeavor is no easy task.
—FRANK PAJARES

Some men are graduated from college cum laude, some are graduated summa cum laude, and some are graduated mirabile dictu.
—WILLIAM HOWARD TAFT

A whaleship was my Yale College and my Harvard.
—HERMAN MELVILLE, FROM *MOBY DICK* (1851)

Four years was enough of Harvard. I still had a lot to learn, but had been given the liberating notion that now I could teach myself.
—John Updike

I think everyone should go to college and get a degree and then spend six months as a bartender and six months as a cabdriver. Then they would really be educated.
—Al McGuire

It is only the ignorant who despise education.
—Publilius Syrus

A college education shows a man how little other people know.
—Thomas Chandler Haliburton

A university education should equip one to entertain three things: a friend, an idea, and one's self.

—Thomas Ehrlich and Juliet Fry, from "Mr. Carnegie's Gift," *Mr. Dooley's Opinions* (1901)

The university is the last remaining platform for national dissent.

—Leon Eisenberg

The real struggle is not between East and West, or capitalism and communism, but between education and propaganda.

—Martin Buber

The function of a University is to enable you to shed details in favor of principles.

—Anonymous

Colleges are like old-age homes, except for the fact that more people die in colleges.

—Bob Dylan, as quoted in *Playboy* (1966)

The bachelor's degree is not the end of the educational journey, but just another milestone.

—Kenneth C. Green, director of the Campus Computing Project

You are educated. Your certification is in your degree. You may think of it as the ticket to the good life. Let me ask you to think of an alternative. Think of it as your ticket to change the world.

—Tom Brokaw

Nine tenths of education is encouragement.
—Anatole France

Ask not what your school can do for you, but what you can do for your school.
—George St. John, as quoted by G. Williams Domhoff in *Who Rules America Now?: A View for the '80s* (1983)

Training is everything. The peach was once a bitter almond; cauliflower is nothing but cabbage with a college education.
—Mark Twain

The business schools reward difficult complex behavior more than simple behavior, but simple behavior is more effective.
—Warren Buffett

No one can look back on his schooldays and say with truth that they were altogether unhappy.
—George Orwell

I believe that in that first year at Dayton High School I learned more about how to work with people and about myself—than any of the thirty-nine years of coaching that followed.
—John Wooden, from his book *My Personal Best* (2004)

It is indeed ironic that we spend our school days yearning to graduate and our remaining days waxing nostalgic about our school days.

—Isabel Waxman, American educator

We have but one rule here and it is that every student must be a gentleman.

—Robert E. Lee, to a student who asked for a copy of the rules at Washington College (now Washington and Lee University)

But this bridge will only take you halfway there— The last few steps you'll have to take alone.

—Shel Silverstein, from "This Bridge," *A Light in the Attic* (1981)

Gentlemen: I have not had your advantages. What poor education I received has been gained at the University of Life.
—HORATIO BOTTOMLEY, IN A SPEECH AT THE OXFORD UNION, 1920

Not art, not books, but life itself is the true basis of . . . education.
—JOHANN HEINRICH PESTALOZZI

We need to be the authors of our own life.
—PETER SENGE, AUTHOR OF *THE DANCE OF CHANGE* (1999)

I may have said the same thing
before . . . But my explanation, I am sure,
will always be different.
—OSCAR WILDE

The best of all teachers, experience.
—PLINY THE YOUNGER

Results! Why, man, I have gotten a
lot of results. I know several thousand
things that won't work.
—THOMAS EDISON

LIFE LESSONS

The only thing experience teaches us is that experience teaches us nothing.
—André Maurois

Experience is a good teacher, but she sends in terrific bills.
—Minna Antrim

Experience is a good school, but the fees are high.
—Heinrich Heine

I believe that education is a process of living and not a preparation for future living.
—John Dewey

Experience keeps a dear school, yet Fools
will learn in no other.
—Benjamin Franklin

A moment's insight is sometimes worth a
life's experience.
—Oliver Wendell Holmes, Sr., from his book *The
Professor at the Breakfast-Table* (1860)

Mr. B's F.A.C.T.S. of Life:
Flexibility
Accountability
Cooperation
Trust
Sincerity
—T. Bogusz

Our life is an apprenticeship to the truth that around every circle another can be drawn.
—Ralph Waldo Emerson

Life is ten percent what happens to me and ninety percent how I react to it.
—Charles Swindoll

It's not the load that breaks you down, it's the way you carry it.
—Lou Holtz

It's kind of fun to do the impossible.
—Walt Disney

Expecting something for nothing is the most popular form of hope.
—Arnold Glasow

Prepare for the unknown by studying how others in the past have coped with the unforeseeable and the unpredictable.

—GEORGE PATTON

Look not mournfully into the past, it comes not back again. Wisely improve the present, it is thine. Go forth to meet the shadowy future without fear and with a manly heart.

—HENRY WADSWORTH LONGFELLOW

First say to yourself what you would be; and then do what you have to do.

—EPICTETUS

Only so much do I know, as I have lived.
Instantly we know whose words are baded
with life, and whose are not.
—RALPH WALDO EMERSON, FROM HIS BOOK
THE AMERICAN SCHOLAR SELF-RELIANCE
COMPENSATION (1837)

Discoveries are often made by not following
instructions; by going off the main road; by
trying the untried.
—FRANK TYGER

The more original a discovery, the
more obvious it seems afterward.
—ARTHUR KOESTLER

The moment a person forms a theory, his imagination sees, in every object, only the traits that favor that theory.
—THOMAS JEFFERSON

The most damaging phrase in the language is "It's always been done that way."
—GRACE MURRAY HOPPER

It is not in the stars to hold our destiny, but in ourselves.
—WILLIAM SHAKESPEARE

Winning isn't everything, but wanting to win is.
—VINCE LOMBARDI

Humans are allergic to change. They love to say, "We've always done it this way." I try to fight that. That's why I have a clock on my wall that runs counter-clockwise.

—GRACE MURRAY HOPPER

There are young people out there cutting raw cocaine with chemicals from the local hardware store . . . and each of these new drugs is more addictive, more deadly, and less costly than the last . . . How is it that we have failed to tap that ingenuity, that sense of experimentation?

—SENATOR KOHL, FROM THE U.S. SENATE HEARING "CRISIS IN MATH AND SCIENCE EDUCATION"

Reinventing the wheel is a process.

—RASHID ELISHA

A talent is formed in stillness, a character in the world's torrent.

—Johann Wolfgang von Goethe

The future is yet full of trial and success. There is happiness to be enjoyed! There is good to be done! Exchange this false life of thine for a true one.

—Nathaniel Hawthorne

The circumstances that surround a man's life are not important. How that man responds to those circumstances is important. His response is the ultimate determining factor between success and failure.

—Booker T. Washington

In leadership, there are no words more important than trust. In any organization, trust must be developed among every member of the team if success is going to be achieved.

—Mike Krzyzewski, college basketball coach

You must understand the whole of life, not just one little part of it. That is why you must read, that is why you must look at the skies, that is why you must sing and dance, and write poems, and suffer, and understand, for all that is life.

—Jiddu Krishnamurti

I really consider life to be like studying. The first thing I look up when I'm out of town is the local museum. You can always continue to learn.

—Sarah Michelle Gellar

You live your life between your ears.
—Bebe Moore Campbell

All of the top achievers I know are life-long learners . . . looking for new skills, insights, and ideas. If they're not learning, they're not growing . . . not moving toward excellence.
—Denis Waitley

We now accept the fact that learning is a lifelong process of keeping abreast of change. And the most pressing task is to teach people how to learn.
—Peter F. Drucker

There is more to life than increasing its speed.
—Gandhi

323

Perhaps the angels who fear to tread where fools rush in used to be fools who rushed in.
—Franklin P. Jones

The very least you can do in your life is to figure out what you hope for. And the most you can do is live inside that hope. Not admire it from a distance but live right in it, under its roof.
—Barbara Kingsolver, from her book *Animal Dreams* (1997)

No matter how deep a study you make, what you really have to rely on is your own intuition and when it comes down to it, you really don't know what's going to happen until you do it.
—Konosuke Matsushita, as quoted in *Matsushita Leadership* (1997)

324

The happiest life is that which constantly exercises and educates what is best in us.
—PHILIP G. HAMERTON, AUTHOR OF *INTELLECTUAL LIFE* (1981)

Most of the most important experiences that truly educate cannot be arranged ahead of time with any precision.
—HAROLD TAYLOR

Time is a great teacher, but unfortunately it kills all its pupils.
—LOUIS HECTOR BERLIOZ

It's never too late to start over, never too late to be happy.
—JANE FONDA

325

If the past cannot teach the present and the father cannot teach the son, then history need not have bothered to go on, and the world has wasted a great deal of time.
—Russell Hoban

We are inheritors of a past that gives us every reason to believe that we will succeed.
—Anonymous

Yesterday is a dream, tomorrow but a vision. But today well lived makes every yesterday a dream of happiness, and every tomorrow a vision of hope. Look well, therefore, to this day.
—Sanskrit proverb

The adult with a capacity for true maturity is one who has grown out of childhood without losing childhood's best traits.
—Joseph Stone

Maturity is not a goal, but rather a process.
—Dr. Leo Buscaglia

Lives of great men all remind us
We can make our lives sublime,
And, departing, leave behind us
Footprints on the sands of time.
—Henry Wadsworth Longfellow

Time, as it grows old, teaches all things.
—Aeschylus

Vague and nebulous is the beginning of all things, but not their end.

—Kahlil Gibran

He would not be ashamed of dying . . . He could be research. A human textbook. Study me in my slow and patient demise. Watch what happens to me. Learn with me.

—Mitch Albom, from his book *Tuesdays with Morrie* (1997)

Times of great calamity and confusion have ever been productive of the greatest minds. The purest ore is produced from the hottest furnace, and the brightest thunderbolt is elicited from the darkest storm.

—Charles Caleb Colton

As we experience the world, so we act.
—R.D. LAING, FROM HIS BOOK *THE POLITICS OF EXPERIENCE* (1967)

We shall never learn to feel and respect our real calling and destiny, unless we have taught ourselves to consider every thing as moonshine, compared with the education of the heart.
—SIR WALTER SCOTT

Learn not only to find what you like, learn to like what you find.
—ANTHONY J. D'ANGELO, FROM HIS BOOK *THE COLLEGE BLUE BOOK* (1995)

If you do not expect it, you will not find the unexpected, for it is hard to find and difficult.

—HERACLITUS

I am always doing that which I cannot do, in order that I may learn how to do it.

—PABLO PICASSO

The things we know best are the things we haven't been taught.

—MARQUIS DE VAUVENARGUES

330

If it be knowledge or wisdom one is seeking, then one had better go direct to the source. And the source is not the scholar or philosopher, not the master, saint, or teacher, but life itself—direct experience of life.

—Henry Miller, from the Preface to *The Books in My Life* (1952)

I like to think of my behavior in the sixties as a "learning experience." Then again, I like to think of anything stupid I've done as a "learning experience." It makes me feel less stupid.

—P. J. O'Rourke, from "Second Thoughts about the Sixties," *Give War a Chance* (1992)

Education is a progressive discovery of our own ignorance.
—WILL DURANT

Experience is not what happens to you. It is what you do with what happens to you.
—ALDOUS HUXLEY

She had some experience of the world, and the capacity for reflection that makes such experience profitable.
—JEAN JACQUES ROUSSEAU, FROM HIS BOOK *CONFESSIONS* (1781)

Our experience is composed rather of illusions lost than of wisdom acquired.
—JOSEPH ROUX, FROM HIS BOOK *MEDITATIONS OF A PARISH PRIEST* (1886)

If you would know the road ahead, ask someone who has traveled it.
—CHINESE PROVERB

Don't be discouraged by failure. It can be a positive experience. Failure is, in a sense, the highway to success, inasmuch as every discovery of what is false leads us to seek earnestly after what is true, and every fresh experience points out some form of error, which we shall afterwards carefully avoid.
—JOHN KEATS

You cannot acquire experience by making experiments. You cannot create experience. You must undergo it.
—ALBERT CAMUS

The important thing in life is not the triumph but the struggle.

—Pierre de Coubertin, historian and founder of the modern Olympic Games

There is no education like adversity.

—Benjamin Disraeli

These then are my last words to you: be not afraid of life. Believe that life is worth living and your belief will help create the fact.

—William James

If you truly want to bless others in your life, you must seek out those experiences that keep you motivated and inspired, and then share them.

—Thomas Kinkade

334

It's okay to make mistakes. Mistakes are our teachers—they help us to learn.
— JOHN BRADSHAW

Tell me and I forget. Show me and I remember. Involve me and I understand.
—CHINESE PROVERB

The essence of intelligence is skill in extracting meaning from everyday experience.
—ANONYMOUS

We learn geology the morning after the earthquake.
—RALPH WALDO EMERSON, FROM "CONSIDERATIONS BY THE WAY," THE CONDUCT OF LIFE (1860)

I have learned silence from the talkative, toleration from the intolerant, and kindness from the unkind; yet, strange, I am ungrateful to these teachers.
—Kahlil Gibran

The main part of intellectual education is not the acquisition of facts but learning how to make facts live.
—Oliver Wendell Holmes

Men must be taught as if you taught them not, And things unknown proposed as things forgot.
—Alexander Pope

There are two types of education. One should teach us how to make a living, and the other how to live.
—JOHN ADAMS

I would rather live in a world where my life is surrounded by mystery than live in a world so small that my mind could comprehend it.
—HENRY EMERSON FOSDICK

You will never stub your toe standing still. The faster you go, the more chance there is of stubbing your toe, but the more chance you have of getting somewhere.
—CHARLES F. KETTERING

If you can spend a perfectly useless afternoon in a perfectly useless manner, you have learned how to live.
—Lin Yutang

You can get help from teachers, but you are going to have to learn a lot by yourself, sitting alone in a room.
—Theodore "Dr. Seuss" Geisel

A fall from the third floor hurts as much as a fall from the hundredth. If I have to fall, may it be from a high place.
—Paulo Coelho

There are three schoolmasters for everybody that will employ them—the senses, intelligent companions, and books.
—Henry Ward Beecher

It is by teaching that we teach ourselves, by relating that we observe, by affirming that we examine, by showing that we look, by writing that we think, by pumping that we draw water into the well.
—Henri-Frédéric Amiel

Give a man a fish and you feed him for a day. Teach him how to fish and you feed him for a lifetime.
—Lao Tzu

The educator must above all understand how to wait; to reckon all effects in the light of the future, not of the present.
—Ellen Key

Too often we give children answers to remember rather than problems to solve.
—Roger Lewin

Come forth into the light of things, let nature be your teacher.
—William Wordsworth

We have to look for routes of power our teachers never imagined, or were encouraged to avoid.
—Thomas Pynchon, from his book *Gravity's Rainbow* (1973)

To live for a long time close to great minds is the best kind of education.
—John Buchan, from his book *Memory Hold-the-Door* (1940)

I studied the lives of great men and famous women; and I found that the men and women who got to the top were those who did the jobs they had in hand, with everything they had of energy and enthusiasm and hard work.
—Harry S. Truman

If I have seen farther than other men, it is because I have stood on the shoulders of giants.
—Isaac Newton

Education is an admirable thing, but it is well to remember from time to time that nothing that is worth knowing can be taught.

—"HTTP://WWW.CYBERNATION.COM/VICTORY/QUOTATIONS/AUTHORS/QUOTES_WILDE_OSCAR.HTML" OSCAR WILDE

The greatest education in the world is watching the masters at work.

—MICHAEL JACKSON

There is a time in every man's education when he arrives at the conviction that envy is ignorance; that imitation is suicide; that he must take himself for better, for worse, as his portion; that though the wide universe is full of good, no kernel of nourishing corn can come to him but through his toil bestowed on that plot of ground which is given to him to till. The power which resides in him is new in nature, and none but he knows what that is which he can do, nor does he know until he has tried.

—RALPH WALDO EMERSON, FROM HIS BOOK *SELF-RELIANCE* (1839)

Inside every problem are the seeds of innovative solutions.

—REED MARKHAM

Wherever we look upon this earth, the opportunities take shape within the problems.

—Nelson A. Rockefeller

The mark of a well-educated person is not necessarily in knowing all the answers, but in knowing where to find them.

—Douglas Everett

It is not enough for me to answer questions; I want to know how to answer the one question that seems to encompass everything I face: What am I here for?

—Abraham Joshua Heschel, from his book *Who Is Man?* (1965)

The day after never we will have an explanation.
—HENRY DAVID THOREAU, FROM HIS JOURNAL DATED NOVEMBER 8, 1857

You are also asking me questions and I hear you, I answer that I cannot answer, you must find out for yourself.
—WALT WHITMAN, FROM HIS POEM "SONG OF MYSELF" (1855)

It is not a question of how much a man knows, but what use he can make of what he knows.
—JOSIAH GILBERT HOLLAND, FROM "SELF-HELP," PLAIN TALKS ON FAMILIAR SUBJECTS (1866)

345

He knows who says: we do not know.
—Upanishads

There is a theory which states that if ever anybody discovers exactly what the universe is for and why it is here, it will instantly disappear and be replaced by something even more bizarre and inexplicable. There is another theory which states that this has already happened.
—Douglas Adams, from his book *The Hitchhiker's Guide to the Galaxy* (1995)

When you want something, all the universe conspires in helping you to achieve it
—Paulo Coelho

The thing always happens that you really believe in; and the belief in a thing makes it happen.
—Frank Loyd Wright

Throughout the centuries there were men who took first steps down new roads armed with nothing but their own vision.
—Ayn Rand

The noblest search is the search for excellence.
—Lyndon B. Johnson

What is now proved was once only imagined.
—WILLIAM BLAKE

When we feel stuck, going nowhere—even starting to slip backward—we may actually be backing up to get a running start.
—DAN MILLMAN, AUTHOR OF *WAY OF THE PEACEFUL WARRIOR* (1980)

Even if I knew that tomorrow the world would go to pieces, I would still plant my apple tree.
—MARTIN LUTHER

Not all who wander are lost.
—J. R. R. TOLKIEN

348

Keep away from people who try to belittle your ambitions. Small people always do that, but the really great make you feel that you, too, can become great.

—MARK TWAIN

The easiest thing in the world is to be you. The most difficult thing to be is what other people want you to be. Don't let them put you in that position.

—DR. LEO BUSCAGLIA

Labor to keep alive in your breast that little spark of celestial fire called conscience.

—GEORGE WASHINGTON

A man should have any number of little aims about which he should be conscious and for which he should have names, but he should have neither name for, nor consciousness concerning, the main aim of his life.
—SAMUEL BUTLER

Friendship is the hardest thing in the world to explain. It's not something you learn in school. But if you haven't learned the meaning of friendship, you really haven't learned anything.
—MUHAMMAD ALI

The best way to know life is to love many things.
—VINCENT VAN GOGH

The best index to a person's character is a) how he treats people who can't do him any good and b) how he treats people who can't fight back.
—ABIGAIL VAN BUREN ("DEAR ABBY")

Character may be manifested in the great moments, but it is made in the small ones.
—PHILLIPS BROOKS

Seek education rather than grades. Seek your best rather than someone else's. Seek friendship rather than acceptance. Seek worth rather than rank. Seek to build rather than to tear down. Seek laughter and love in spite of pain and you will have learned to live.
—JAQUI SHEEHAN

All paths are the same. They lead nowhere. They are paths going through the brush or into the brush or under the brush. "Does this path have a heart?" is the only question. If it does, then the path is good. If it doesn't, then it is of no use.

—Carlos Castaneda

He who cherishes a beautiful vision, a lofty ideal in his heart, will one day realize it.

—James Allen

I think everyone should experience defeat at least once during their career. You learn a lot from it.

—Lou Holtz

Go ahead and do the impossible. It's worth the look on the faces of those who said you couldn't.
—WALTER BAGEHOT

We cannot do everything at once, but we can do something at once.
—CALVIN COOLIDGE

People look at you and me to see what they are supposed to be. And, if we don't disappoint them, maybe, just maybe, they won't disappoint us.
—WALT DISNEY

Do not let anyone look down on you because you are young, but set an example for all believers in speech, in life, in love, in faith and in purity.

—St. Paul

It is our choices, Harry, that show what we truly are, far more than our abilities.

—J. K. Rowling

If I opened a film school, I would make everyone earn their tuition themselves by working . . . out where there is real life. Earn it as a bouncer in a sex club or as a warden in a lunatic asylum . . . That makes you more of a filmmaker than three years of film school.

—Werner Herzog

354

Whenever you are asked if you can do a job, tell 'em "Certainly, I can!" Then get busy and find out how to do it.
—THEODORE ROOSEVELT

Hide not your talents, they for use were made. What's a sun-dial in the shade?
—BENJAMIN FRANKLIN

One is always a long way from solving a problem until one actually has the answer.
—STEPHEN HAWKING

Go to the edge of the cliff and jump off. Build your wings on the way down.
—RAY BRADBURY

355

Nothing is particularly hard if you divide it into small jobs.
—HENRY FORD

Luctor et Emergo ("I struggle and I come through").
—MOTTO OF NOTRE DAME COLLEGE OF SASKATCHEWAN

Our deepest fear is not that we are inadequate. Our deepest fear is that we are powerful beyond measure. It is our light, not our darkness that most frightens us . . . Your playing small doesn't serve the world.
—NELSON MANDELA

Failure should be our teacher, not our undertaker. Failure is delay, not defeat. It is a temporary detour, not a dead end. Failure is something we can avoid only by saying nothing, doing nothing, and being nothing.
—DENIS WAITLEY

Ah, but a man's reach should exceed his grasp, or what's a heaven for?
—ROBERT BROWNING

Don't bunt. Aim out of the ballpark.
—DAVID OGILVY

The difference between perseverance and obstinacy is that one often comes from a strong will, and the other from a strong won't.
—HENRY WARD BEECHER

We all have ability. The difference is how we use it.

—STEVIE WONDER

The best place to succeed is where you are with what you have.

—CHARLES SCHWAB

Effective people are not problem-minded; they're opportunity minded. They feed opportunities and starve problems.

—STEPHEN COVEY

All growth depends upon activity. There is no development physically or intellectually without effort, and effort means work.

—CALVIN COOLIDGE

Think of yourself as on the threshold of unparalleled success. A whole clear, glorious life lies before you. Achieve! Achieve!
—ANDREW CARNEGIE

You don't become enormously successful without encountering some really interesting problems.
—MARK VICTOR HANSEN, AMERICAN MOTIVATIONAL SPEAKER AND CO-CREATOR OF THE "CHICKEN SOUP FOR THE SOUL" BOOK SERIES

Build up your weaknesses until they become your strong points.
—KNUTE ROCKNE

One can succeed at almost anything for which he has enthusiasm.

—CHARLES SCHWAB

Success is the sum of small efforts, repeated day in and day out.

—ROBERT COLLIER

I attribute my success to this—I never gave or took any excuse.

—FLORENCE NIGHTINGALE

I therefore admonish my students in Europe and America: Don't aim at success— the more you aim at it and make it a target, the more you are going to miss it. For success, like happiness, cannot be pursued; it must ensue.

—VIKTOR FRANKL

Success does not consist in never making blunders, but in never making the same one a second time.

—Josh Billings

Aim for success, not perfection. Never give up your right to be wrong, because then you will lose the ability to learn new things and move forward with your life. Remember that fear always lurks behind perfectionism.

—David M. Burns

I learned this, at least, by my experiment: that if one advances confidently in the direction of his dreams, and endeavors to live the life which he has imagined, he will meet with a success unexpected in common hours.

—Henry David Thoreau

Success is that old ABC—ability, breaks, and courage.

—Charles Luckman

My great concern is not whether you have failed, but whether you are content with your failure.

—Abraham Lincoln

The secret of success in life is for a man to be ready for his opportunity when it comes.
—Benjamin Disraeli

The talent of success is nothing more than doing what you can do, well.
—Henry Wadsworth Longfellow

Far more crucial than what we know or do not know is what we do not want to know.
—Eric Hoffer, from his book *The Passionate State of Mind: And Other Aphorisms* (1954)

If you find a path with no obstacles, it probably doesn't lead anywhere.
—Frank A. Clark

Sometimes it is more important to discover what one cannot do, than what one can do.
—Lin Yutang

Because a thing seems difficult for you, do not think it impossible for anyone to accomplish.
—Marcus Aurelius

When you do a thing, do it with all you might. Put your whole soul into it. Stamp it with your own personality . . . Nothing great was ever achieved without enthusiasm.
—Ralph Waldo Emerson

If you want to increase your success rate, double your failure rate.
—THOMAS WATSON, SR., FOUNDER OF IBM

There is only one thing that makes a dream impossible to achieve: the fear of failure.
—PAULO COELHO

All our dreams can come true, if we have the courage to pursue them.
—WALT DISNEY

Always do more than is required of you.
—GEORGE PATTON

Do a little more each day than you think
you can.
—Lowell Thomas

Talent is like electricity. We don't understand
electricity. We use it.
—Maya Angelou, as quoted in *Black Women Writers at Work* (1983)

Goals are the fuel in the furnace of achievement.
—Brian Tracy, motivational coach and author, from his book *Eat that Frog*

They will rise highest who strive for the highest
place.
—Latin proverb

Many great actions are committed in small struggles.

—Victor Hugo, from *Les Misérables*

If you can't accept losing, you can't win.

—Vince Lombardi

Victory belongs to the most persevering.

—Napoleon Bonaparte

If you aren't going all the way, why go at all?

—Joe Namath

Nothing can stop the man with the right mental attitude from achieving his goal; nothing on earth can help the man with the wrong mental attitude.

—Thomas Jefferson

367

YOUNG PEOPLE AND
NEW GENERATIONS

What's amazing is, if young people understood how doing well in school makes the rest of their life so much more interesting, they would be more motivated. It's so far away in time that they can't appreciate what it means for their whole life.
—BILL GATES

Our communities benefit from healthy, productive, well-prepared young people.
—JANE FONDA

Education exposes young people to a broader world, a world full of opportunity and hope.
—CHRISTINE GREGOIRE

Dear young people, do not bury your talents, the gifts that god has given you! Do not be afraid to dream of great things!
—POPE FRANCIS

Don't lie to anyone, but particularly don't lie to millennials. They just know. They can smell it. When you credit teenagers with intelligence and emotional sophistication, they respond intelligently and with emotional sophistication.
—JOHN GREEN

Millennials are often portrayed as apathetic, disinterested, tuned out and selfish. None of those adjectives describe the Millennials I've been privileged to meet and work with.
—CHELSEA CLINTON

If young people had love, hope, true education, the arts, full and meaningful lives they wouldn't join gangs.

—Luis J. Rodriguez

Young people need models, not critics.

—John Wooden

My message, especially to young people, is to have courage to think differently, courage to invent, to travel the unexplored path, courage to discover the impossible and to conquer the problems and succeed.

—Abdul Kalam

Young people should be at the forefront of global change and innovation. Empowered, they can be key agents for development and peace. If, however, they are left on society's margins, all of us will be impoverished. Let us ensure that all young people have every opportunity to participate fully in the lives of their societies.

—KOFI ANNAN

Our young people look up to us. Let us not let them down. Our young people need us. Saving them will make heroes of us all.

—GALE SAYERS

Those who control what young people are taught, and what they experience—what they see, hear, think, and believe—will determine the future course for the nation.
—JAMES DOBSON

What should young people do with their lives today? Many things, obviously. But the most daring thing is to create stable communities in which the terrible disease of loneliness can be cured.
—KURT VONNEGUT

We must view young people not as empty bottles to be filled, but as candles to be lit.
—ROBERT H. SHAFFER

Give young people a greater voice. They are the future and they are much wiser than we give them credit for.
—Desmond Tutu

I would tell young people to start where they are with what they have and that the secret of a big success is starting with a small success and dreaming bigger and bigger dreams.
—John H. Johnson

There's nothing I believe in more strongly than getting young people interested in science and engineering, for a better tomorrow, for all humankind.
—Bill Nye

Psychology, unlike chemistry, unlike algebra, unlike literature, is an owner's manual for your own mind. It's a guide to life. What could be more important than grounding young people in the scientific information that they need to live happy, healthy, productive lives? To have good relationships?

—DANIEL GOLDSTEIN

Vocational education programs have made a real difference in the lives of countless young people nationwide; they build self-confidence and leadership skills by allowing students to utilize their unique gifts and talents.

—CONRAD BURNS

Young people at universities study to achieve knowledge and not to learn a trade. We must all learn how to support ourselves, but we must also learn how to live. We need a lot of engineers in the modern world, but we do not want a world of modern engineers.

—Winston Churchill

Young people are capable, when aroused, of bringing down the towers of oppression and raising the banners of freedom.

—Nelson Mandela

Encouraging young people to believe in themselves and find their own voice whether it's through writing, drama, or art is so important in giving young people a sense of self-worth.

—Michael Morpurgo

Help young people. Help small guys. Because small guys will be big. Young people will have the seeds you bury in their minds, and when they grow up, they will change the world.

—Jack Ma

I believe that young people are looking for answers to the big questions just like everyone else, and that they respect intelligent comment to help guide them through tough times.

—Bill Kurtis

If everything had already been done, there would be nothing left for young people to accomplish. There are always going to be people who run faster, jump higher, dive deeper, and come up drier.

—Darrell Royal

378

I tell young people to prepare themselves as best they can for a world that grows more challenging every day—get the best education they can, and couple that education with real-life experience in social justice work.
—Julian Bond

What is a coach? We are teachers. Educators. We have the same obligations as all teachers, except we probably have more influence over young people than anybody but their families. And, in a lot of cases, more than their families.
—Joe Paterno

I would so much like young people to have a sense of the gift that they are. Not many of them feel like that.
—John Denver

It is essential that we enable young people to see themselves as participants in one of the most exciting eras in history, and to have a sense of purpose in relation to it.

—Nelson Rockefeller

The most common thing I find is very brilliant, acute, young people who want to become writers but they are not writing. You know, they really badly want to write a book but they are not writing it. The only advice I can give them is to just write it, get to the end of it. And, you know, if it's not good enough, write another one.

—Teju Cole

There's no excuse for the young people not knowing who the heroes and heroines are or were.

—Nina Simone

Hopefully, young people will see that you can be young and make the sacrifices to follow your dreams.
—Tinie Tempah

One of the great things about young people is that they do question, that they do care deeply about justice, and that they have open minds.
—Zack de la Rocha

Teachers are our greatest public servants; they spend their lives educating our young people and shaping our Nation for tomorrow.
—Solomon Ortiz

I do genuinely believe that young people who play sport at a competitive level, sensibly controlled, sensibly organised, that has to be a good thing. It will teach them to win, it will teach them to lose with dignity and magnanimity—all the things you want. It's a pretty good metaphor for life.

—Sebastian Coe

The capacity of young people to persevere, even under the most adverse conditions, never ceases to amaze me.

—Jane Fonda

I believe in recovery, and I believe that as a role model I have the responsibility to let young people know that you can make a mistake and come back from it.

—Ann Richards

We should never discourage young people from dreaming dreams.
—Lenny Wilkens

Technology is permeating every single thing we do . . . and to the extent that we can better expose our young people to all the different ways that technology can be used, not just for video games or toys, we're planning for the future.
—Marc Morial

Young people are just as attracted to the truth as they are convenience and expediency.
—Pope Francis

America needs young people to be inspired to choose sacrifice over greed.
—JESSE JACKSON

Young people have so much more power than they tend to think to be able to affect politics.
—JOHN F. KERRY

A good education is the most important gift we can give our young people.
—NICOLA STURGEON

You can't be afraid to not have everything figured out. There's too much pressure on young people today to have it all figured out when they're in college.
—CHARLIE TROTTER

384

Keeping young people away from Shakespeare
is like removing a link to their humanness.
—Tim Crouch

When something startlingly new comes up,
young people, especially, seize it. You can't
complain about that.
—M. H. Abrams

Trust the young. Young people have a
lot to contribute, but generation after
generation, those who reach power
protect that power rather than teach
others how to attain it. I resolved
that if I ever became successful, I
would trust the young.
—Guy Laliberte

I think it's important to give young people the freedom to follow their ideas and pursue their interests.

—Venkatraman Ramakrishnan

In addition to exploring imaginative worlds, I believe that young people should have access to reading material that validates their life, that gives them a sense of identity—to be able to read text that chimes with their own world, corrals thoughts, and connects with the emotional conflicts of growing up.

—Theresa Breslin

Young people are fitter to invent than to judge; fitter for execution than for counsel; and more fit for new projects than for settled business.

—Francis Bacon

We need to tell young people that America was built by men and women of all colors and that the future of this country is dependent on the participation of all of our citizens.

—Walter Dean Myers

The extreme sophistication of modern technology—wonderful though its benefits are—is, ironically, an impediment to engaging young people with basics: with learning how things work.

— John W. Gardner

Those Quoted

Those Quoted

Barnes, Julian
Barrie, J.M.
Barron, Frank
Barry, Dave
Barrymore, Ethel
Baruch, Bernard
Barzun, Jacques
Batten, Joe
Basho, Matsuo
Bayer, Ernest
Beard, Charles A.
Beattie, Bill
Beattie, James
Beatty, Cameron
Becker, Carl Lotus
Bedford, Clay P.
Beecher, Henry Ward
Beerbohm, Max
Bejar, Hada
Belcher, Gerald
Bellow, Saul
Benedict, Francis C.
Benevento, Mike
Bennett, Alan
Bennett, Dan
Bennis, Warren G.
Bennett, William J.
Benson, A. C.
Bergson, Henri
Berlioz, Louis Hector
Berman, Louis A.
Bernbach, Bill
Bernard, Claude
Bernstein, Al
Bernstein, Leonard
Berra, Yogi

Berston, Hyman
Bertin, Eugene P.
Bethune, Mary McLeod
Bhagavatam, Srimad
Bhave, Vinoba
Bierce, Ambrose
Billings, John
Billings, Josh
Birnbach, Lisa
Blake, William
Blanchard, Kenneth
Blishen, Edward
Bloch, Arthur
Bloom, Allan
Bloom, Harold
Bly, Robert
Boatroux, Pierre
Bogusz, T.
Bohr, Niels
Bok, Derek
Bombeck, Erma
Bonaparte, Napoleon
Bond, Julian
Bonhoeffer, Dietrich
Boorstin, Daniel J.
Borges, Jorge Luis
Bott, Raoul
Botstein, Leon
Bottomley, Horatio
Bourget, Paul
Bourne, Alec
Bovee, Christian Nestell
Bowen, Elizabeth
Bowman, Scotty
Boyden, Frank L.
Boyer, Ernest L.

Boyse, J. F.
Brackell, Fogg
Bradbury, Ray
Bradshaw, John
Breslin, Theresa
Brewster, Kingman
Brilliant, Ashleigh
Brinkmann, Tracy
Bristol, Claude M.
Brock, William E.
Brodie, Fawn M.
Brodsky, Joseph
Brokaw, Tom
Bronfenbrenner, Uri
Bronowski, Jacob
Brookfield, Stephen
Brooks, Phillips
Brooks, Phyllis
Broughan, Henry Peter
Brown, A. Whitney
Brown, Jr., H. Jackson
Brown, Henry Billings
Brown, John Mason
Brown, J. A. C.
Browning, Elizabeth Barett
Browning, Robert
Bruce, Lenny
Bruner, Jerome S.
Bryan, William Lowe
Buber, Martin
Buchan, John
Buck, Pearl S.
Buckley, Kim Walkley
Buddha
Buffett, Warren
Bulwer-Lytton, Edward

Those Quoted

Burchfield, Robert
Burckhardt, Jacob
Burgess, Anthony
Burke, Edmund
Burnham, George P.
Burns, Conrad
Burns, George
Burns, Robert
Burroughs, John
Buscaglia, Dr. Leo
Bush, Barbara
Butler, David
Butler, Nicolas Murray
Butler, Samuel
Butterfield, Sir Herbert
Buttons, Red
Buzzell, Robert
Byatt, A.S.
Byrne, Robert

C

Caballero, James
Caen, Herb
Caesar, Julius
Caldicott, Helen
Callabro, Brian
Callas, Maria
Campbell, Bebe Moore
Campbell, Joseph
Camus, Albert
Canetti, Elias
Canfield, Jack
Capouya, Emile
Capp, Al
Capra, Frank
Carayol, Rene
Careb, Albert

Carlin, George
Carlson, David
Carlyle, Thomas
Carnegie, Dale
Carmichael, J.W.
Carolus S. J., John
Carr, Edward Hallett
Carroll, Lewis
Carruthers, Thomas
Carson, Rachel
Carter, Brad
Carter, Hodding
Carter, Rosalynn
Cary, Joyce
Castaneda, Carlos
Cather, Willa
Cecil, Richard
Cervantes, Miguel de
Chamfort, Nicolas
Chambers, Paul
Chandler, Raymond
Channing, William Ellery
Chapin, Edwin H.
Chapman, George
Chapman, John Jay
Charles, Platt
Chase, Alexander
Chaucer, Geoffrey
Chavez, Cesar
Chekhov, Anton
Chesterton, G. K.
Childre, Doc
Chopra, Deepak
Christie, Agatha
Chung, Kuan
Churchill, Winston
Ciardi, John

Cicero, Marcus T.
Clafford, Patricia
Clark, Muriel
Clark, Ron
Clark, Septima Poinsette
Clarke, Arthur C.
Clarke, John
Cleaver, Eldridge
Clemenceau, Georges
Clinton, Bill
Clinton, Chelsea
Clyde. R. D.
Cochrane, Peter
Cocteau, Jean
Codell, Esmé Raji
Coe, Sebastian
Coelho, Paulo
Cohen, David
Cohen, Marshall
Cole, Joanna
Cole, Teju
Coleridge, Samuel Taylor
Colette
Collie, G. Norman
Collier, Robert
Collins, Marva
Colorose, Barbara
Colton, Charles Caleb
Combs, Arthur
Comenius, Jan Amos
Commager, Henry Steele
Conant, James B.
Condorcet
Confucius
Conger, Lesley
Connors, Jimmy
Conroy, Pat

Those Quoted

Dürrenmatt, Friedrich
Dylan, Bob

E
Ealy, C. Diane
Eckhart, Johannes
Eco, Umberto
Edelman, Marian Wright
Edison, Thomas
Edman, Irwin
Edmundon, Mark
Edward, Henry
Edwards, Bob
Edwards, Otis C.
Edwards, Tyron
Ehrenburg, Ilya
Ehrhard, Joseph
Ehrlich, Thomas
Eichbaum, Wilhelm Lange
Einstein, Albert
Eisenberg, Leon
Eisenberg, Rebecca L.
Eisenhower, Dwight D.
Eisner, Elliot
Eldridge, Paul
Eliot, Charles W.
Eliot, George
Eliot, T.S.
Elisha, Rashid
Ellis, Havelock
Ellis, S.G.
Ellul, Jacques
Emerson, Ralph Waldo
Ephron, Nora
Epictetus
Epicurus
Erasmus

Erikson, Erik
Ervin, Sam
Esar, Evan
Escalante, Jaime
Escher, M.C.
Esquith, Rafe
Estrada, Ignacio
Euclid
Euripides
Evans, George
Evans, Mari
Everett, Douglas
Everett, Edward
Everett, J. D.

F
Fairley, Grant
Faraday, Michael
Feather, William
Feiman-Nemser, Sharon
Ferguson, Marilyn
Feyerabend, Paul Karl
Fielding, Henry
Fields, W.C.
Fincher, Cameron
Fischer, Martin M.
Fitzgerald, F. Scott
Fitzgerald, Penelope
Fitz-Gibbon, Bernice
Fitzwater, Ivan Welton
Flaubert, Gustave
Fleming, John V.
Folb, Josh
Fonda, Jane
Forbes, B. C.
Forbes, Malcolm S.
Ford, Henry

Forman, Max
Forster, E. M.
Fosdick, Henry Emerson
France, Anatole
Frankl, Viktor
Franklin, Benjamin
Freire, Paulo
French, Marilyn
Freud, Anna
Freud, Martin
Freud, Sigmund
Friedenburg, Edgar
Friedman, Milton
Fromm, Erich
Frost, Robert
Froude, James Anthony
Frumkes, Lewis B.
Fry, Juliet
Frye, Northrop
Fuess, Claude M.
Fugal, Lavina Christensen
Fulghum, Robert
Fullan, Michael
Fuller, Buckminster
Fuller, Margaret
Fuller, Thomas
Futrell, Mary Hatwood

G
Gabirol, Ibn
Gaisford, Thomas
Galbraith, John Kenneth
Galilei, Galileo
Galsworthy, John
Gampopa
Gandhi, Indira
Gandhi, Mahatma

Those Quoted

Gardeneer, Jim
Gardner, David P.
Gardner, John W.
Garfield, James A.
Garr, William
Gasparik, Barbara
Gates, Bill
Gates, Tom
Gati, Jean
Gaus, Carl Friedrich
Geiger, Keith
Geisel, Theodore
   "Dr. Seuss"
Gellar, Sarah Michelle
Gerhardie, William
Gerhart, Susan
Geyl, Pieter
Giamatti, A. Bartlett
Gibbon, Edward
Gibran, Kahlil
Gibson, Althea
Gide, Andre
Gilchrist, Ellen
Gildersleeve, Virginia
Gingrich, Newt
Ginott, Haim
Glasgow, Ellen
Glasow, Arnold
Glasser, William
Godwin, Gail
Goldberg, Whoopi
Golding, William
Goldman, Emma
Goldman, Katy
Goldstein, Daniel
Goldsmith, Oliver
Goldwyn, Sam

Goodard, John
Goode, Ruth
Goodman, Paul
Gould, Steven Jay
Gove, Philip Babcock
Gowin, D. B.
Gracián, Baltasar
Graffito
Graham, Michelle L.
Graham, Paul
Gray, Paul E.
Gray, Thomas
Gray, William H.
Green, John
Green, Kenneth C.
Greenspan, Alan
Gregoire, Christine
Gress, Robert
Grimke, Angelina
Gruenberg, Sidonie
Guardino, Karen
Gudder, S.
Guedalla, Philip
Gustavson, Carl G.
Guthrie, Woody

H

Hahn, Kurt
Hainstock, Elizabeth G.
Halberstam, David
Hale, E. E.
Haley, Gail
Haley, Sir William
Haliburton, Thomas
   Chandler
Halmos, Paul
Halsey, Margaret

Hamerton, Philip G.
Hamilton, Edith
Hamilton, Jane
Hamilton, Robert M.
Hammerstein II, Oscar
Hampton, Judy
Hand, Learned
Hanks, Tom
Hannah, John A.
Hansen, Mark Victor
Hardwick, Elizabeth
Hardy, G.H.
Hardy, Thomas
Hargraves, Andy
Harper, Frances Ellen
   Watkins
Harrington, Sir John
Harris, Sidney J.
Harris, Townsend
Hart, B.H. Liddell
Haskins, Henry S.
Haughton, Rosemary
Hawking, Stephen
Hawthorne, Nathaniel
Hay, Ian
Hay, LeRoy E.
Hayes, Helen
Hayes, John R.
Hazlitt, William
Heaviside, Oliver
Hegel, Georg
Hein, Piet
Heine, Heinrich
Heinlein, Robert
Helmers, Dane
Helps, Arthur
Helvetius, Claude Adrien

Those Quoted

Hemingway, Ernest
Hena, Ibrahim
Hendrix, Jimi
Heraclitus
Herbert, Bob
Herbert, George
Herbert, Sir Alan
Herold, Don
Herrigel, Eugen
Hershey, Lenore
Hershey, Lewis B.
Herstein, I.N.
Herzog, Werner
Heschel, Abraham Joshua
Hesse, Hermann
Hibben, Dr. John G.
Hifler, Jane Sequichie
Highet, Gilbert
Hildebrand, Joel H.
Hill, Napoleon
Hitchcock, Alfred
Hitchcock, R. D.
Hitler, Adolf
Hoban, Russell
Hodge, A.A.
Hoffer, Eric
Hofstadter, Richard
Hogerson, Jeremy
Holder, Geoffrey
Holland, Josiah Gilbert
Holmes, J. A.
Holt, John
Holt, Henry
Holtby, Winifred
Holtz, Lou
Holzer, Madeline Fuchs

Homer
Hood, Paxton
Hooker, Michael K.
Hooks, Bell
Hoover, Herbert
Hope, Anthony
Hopkins, Tom
Hopper, Grace Murray
Horace
Horner, Martina
Horton, Miles
Houseman, A.E.
Houston, Sam
Howard, Alan
Howe, Edgar Watson
Howe II, Howard
Howell, James
Howells, William Dean
Huang-Po
Hubbard, Elbert
Hubbard, Kin
Hufstedler, Shirley
Hughes, Richard
Hugo, Victor
Hulbert, Harold S.
Huneker, James Gibbons
Hunter, Madeline
Hutchins, Robert
Huxley, Aldous
Huxley, Thomas

I

Iacocca, Lee
Illich, Ivan
Ingersoll, Robert Green
Inman, Reverend E.

Irving, John
Irving, Washington
Irwin, Steve
Ivins, Molly

J

Jackson, Andrew
Jackson, Holbrook
Jackson, Jesse
Jackson, Michael
Jackson, Wendy
Jacobi, Carl
James, Anna
James, William
Jefferson, Thomas
Jervis, Robert
Johannot, Louis
Johnson, Claudia Alta
  Taylor "Lady Bird"
Johnson, David
Johnson, Earvin "Magic"
Johnson, John H.
Johnson, Lyndon B.
Johnson, Kenneth G.
Johnson, Samuel
Jones, Charles T.
Jones, Franklin P.
Jones, James Earl
Jonson, Ben
Jordan, Barbara
Jordan, David Star
Joubert, Joseph
Jovanovich, William
Jowett, Benjamin
Joyce, Bruce
Joyce, James

Those Quoted

Jung, Carl
Juster, Norman
Juvenal

K
Kafka, Franz
Kahn, Hannah
Kaiser, Henry J.
Kalam, Abdul
Kant, Immanuel
Kaufman, Bel
Kazin, Alfred
Keats, John
Keeney, Barnaby C.
Keillor, Garrison
Keller, Helen
Keller, James
Kelly, John
Kelly, Melissa Brooks
Kelly, William M.
Kemeny, John
Kempis, Thomas À.
Kennan, George F.
Kennedy, John F.
Kepes, Gyorgy
Keppel, Francis
Kerouac, Jack
Kerr, Clark
Kerr, Jean
Kerry, John F.
Kettering, Charles F.
Key, Ellen
Keyes, Jr., Ken
Keynes, John
  Maynard
Keyser, Maggie

Kidder, Tracy
Kieran, John
Kierkegaard, Søren
Killian, James R.
King, B. B.
King, Florence
King George VI
King, Jr., Martin Luther
King, Stephen
Kingdon, Frank
Kingsley, Charles
Kingsolver, Barbara
Kingston, Maxine Hong
Kinkade, Thomas
Kiole, Earl
Kipling, Rudyard
Kirk, Grayson
Kissinger, Henry
Kitt, Eartha
Kizlik, R. J.
Kline, Morris
Knight, Bobby
Koch, Edward
Koestler, Arthur
Kohl, Herbert
Kohn, Alfie
Korzybski, Alfred
Kossuth, Louis
Kovalevskaya,
  Sophia
Kozol, Jonathan
Kretschmer, Ernst
Krishna
Krishnamurti, Jiddu
Kronenberger, Louis
Krzyzewski, Mike

Kubrick, Stanley
Kurtis, Bill
Kyi, Aung San Suu

L
L'Engle, Madeleine
Lady Montagu
Laertius, Diogenes
Laing, R. D.
Laliberte, Guy
Lamb, Charles
Land, Dr. Edwin
Landers, Ann
Landor, Walter Savage
Langor, Susanne K.
Lao, Marvin T.
Lara, Adair
Larmer, Paul
Larson, Doug
Lasorda, Tommy
Law, Vernon
Lawrence, D. H.
Le Bon, Gustave
Le Guin, Ursula K.
Leacock, Stephen
Leary, Timothy
LeBlond, Ray
Lebowitz, Fran
Lec, Stanislaw J.
Lederman, Leon M.
Lee, Bruce
Lee, Harper
Lee, Laurence
Lee, Robert E.
Leibniz
Lenin, Vladimir

Those Quoted

Leopardi, Giacomo
LeShan, Edna
Lessing, Doris
Lessinger, Leon
Lester, Howard
Lester, Julius
Levi, Eliphas
Levin, Henry M.
Levine, Barbara
Levinson, Leonard Lewis
Levinson, Sam
Lewin, Roger
Lewis, C. S.
Lewis, Michael
Lewis, Sinclair
Lezotte, Larry
Lichtenberg,
    Georg Christoph
Lieberman, Ann
Lillard, Paula Polk
Lincoln, Abraham
Lindbergh, Ann Morrow
Lindner, Robert
Linnaeus, Carolus
Linzey, Andrew
Lions, Virgin
Lipman, Walter
Locke, John
Lodge, David
Lombardi, Vince
Lomrboso, Cesare
London, Jack
Longfellow, Henry
    Wadsworth
Lord Byron
Lord Chesterfield

Lougbrane, John P.
Lovelock, James
Lowell, Albott Lawrence
Lowell, Amy
Lowell, James Russell
Lubbock, John
Lucas, George
Luckman, Charles
Lujack, Larry
Lukas, Wayne
Luther, Martin

M

Ma, Jack
MacCready, Paul
MacDiarmid, Hugh
MacDonald, Ross
MacGilpin, Greg
MacInnes, Helen
MacLeish, Archibald
MacManus, Seumas
MacMillan, Harold
McAdoo, William G.
McColl Jr., Hugh
McGinnis, A.L.
McGranaghan, Mark
McKenziem, E.C.
Macaulay, Thomas B.
Macomber, Melissa
Macomber sisters
Madden, John
Madison, James
Madwed, Sidney
Maeterlinck, Maurice
Maher, Bill
Mai, Delissa L.

Malcolm X
Mallarme, Stephane
Malloy, Terry
Malone, Dudley Field
Mandela, Nelson
Mankiewicz, Frank
Mann, Horace
Mann, Thomas
Manske, Fred A.
Marissa, Agustin
Markham, Reed
Marquis, Don
Marquis of Halifax
Marriott, J. Willard
Marshall, Peter
Marshall, Sybil
Marshall, Thurgood
Martin, Everett Dean
Martin, Judith
Martineau, Harriet
Marx, Groucho
Maslow, Abraham
Massinger, Philip
Masterman, J. C.
Mathesis, Adrian
Matsushita, Konosuke
Matthew 15:14
Maugham, W. Somerset
Maurois, André
Max, D. T.
May, Lola
Mayor, Federico
Mays, Benjamin
McAuliffe, Christa
McCarty, Meladee
McCord, David

McEdelman, John
McGraw, Dr. Phil
McGuire, Al
McKay, David O.
McLaughlin, Mignon
McLuhan, Marshall
McTamaney, Catherine
McWade, Meredith
McWilliams, Candia
McWilliams, Peter
Mead, Margaret
Mears, Henrietta
Medick, Jean
Meerloo, Joost A. M.
Meier, Deborah
Melby, Ernest
Melville, Herman
Mencken, H. L.
Menninger, Karl
Mercier, Louis
Merton, Paul
Michel, John
Michelangelo
Michener, James A.
Mill, John Stuart
Miller, Alice Duer
Miller, Henry
Millikan, Robert A.
Millman, Dan
Milne, A. A.
Milton, John
Mingus, Charles
Minsky, Marvin
Mistral, Gabriela
Mitchell, Maria
Mittenthal, Sue

Mizner, Wilson
Moats, Louisa
Molière
Montague, Ashley
Montaigne
Montapert, Alfred A.
Montesquieu
Montessori, Maria
Moore, Eliakim H.
Moore, Gordon
Moore, Thomas
Moravia, Alberto
Morgan, Arthur E.
Morgan, Barbara
Morgan, Brian
Morgan, Charles
Morgan, J.P.
Morial, Marc
Morley, Christopher
Morley, John
Morley, Robert
Morpurgo, Michael
Morris, James W.
Morrison, Toni
Moser, Sir Claude
Moskowitz, Faye
Mother Teresa
Muhammad
Muhammad-Earl,
    Dr. Kimberly
Muir, John
Mumford, Lewis
Munro, H. H. (Saki)
Murphy, Patricia
Murrow, Edward R.
Musgrave, Story

Myers, Joyce A.
Myers, Walter Dean

N
Nabokov, Vladimir
Nader, Ralph
Nagel, Greta K.
Naipaul, V.S.
Namath, Joe
Nance, W. A.
Natanson, Maurice
National Conference
    on Higher Education,
    1964
Neal, Patricia
Neil, Humphrey B.
Neill, Rolfe
Neblette, C. B.
Nelson, Bob
Nero, Howard
Neufeld, Barbara
Newman, John Henry
    Cardinal
Newman, Judith
Newman, Lewis I.
Newton, Isaac
New York City
    Board of Education
    Poster
Niemann, Scott D.
Niemeyer, John
Nietzsche, Friedrich
Nin, Anais
Noddings, Nel
Nolte, Dorothy Law
Norris, Kathleen

Northcote, James
Nye, Bill
Nyquist, Ewald B.

O
O'Connor, Flannery
O'Malley, Austin
O'Rourke, P. J.
O'Sullivan, John
Oates, Joyce Carol
Ogilvy, David
Oguntimehin, Ropo
Ohanian, Susan
Olsen, Merlin
Onassis, Jacqueline
    Kennedy
Oppenheimer, Robert
Orben, Robert
Ortega y Gasset, José
Ortiz, Solomon
Orton, William
Orwell, George
Osborne, Joan
Osler, Sir William
Ovid

P
Page, Larry
Paine, Thomas
Pajares, Frank
Palmer, George Herbert
Palmer, Parker J.
Pandit, Vijaya Lakshmi
Papert, Seymour
Paraseghian, Ara
Pareto, Vilfredo
Parker, Dorothy

Parker, Theodore
Pascal, Blaise
Pasteur, Louis
Paterno, Joe
Patton, George S.
Pauling, Linus
Peale, Norman Vincent
Pearson, Hesketh
Peck, Carrie
Penn, William
Percy, Walker
Perelman, Bob
Pericles
Perls, Fritz
Perry, Bliss
Pestalozzi, Johann
    Heinrich
Peter, Laurence J.
Petronius
Phaedrus
Philips, Emo
Phillips, Bob
Phillips, Wendell
Phillpotts, Eden
Philo
Piaget, Jean
Picasso, Pablo
Pierce, Lorne
Pinker, Stephen
Pirsig, Robert M.
Plato
Pleacher, David
Pliny the Elder
Pliny the Younger
Plutarch
Poisson, Simeon
Polya, George

Polyak, Steve
Poole, Mary Pettibone
Pope, Alexander
Pope Francis
Porter, Sylvia
Portman, Natalie
Postman, Neil
Potter, Beatrix
Pound, Ezra
Pratt, Richard
Priestly, John Boynton
Priestly, Joseph
Pritchett, V.S.
Prochnow, Herbet
Protheroe, Nancy
Purkey, William
Pusey, Nathan M.
Pynchon, Thomas
Pythagoras

Q
Quayle, Dan
Queen Victoria
Quindlen, Anna
Quinn, Donald D.
Quintilian

R
Rabelais, François
Ramakrishnan,
    Venkatraman
Rand, Ayn
Raphael, Sally Jesse
Rashi
Rassias, John A.
Rather, Dan
Rau, Johannes

Those Quoted

Simonides
Simpson, Alan
Singer, Ira
Sister Evangelist
Sizer, Theodore R.
Smith, Adam
Skinner, B. F.
Smith, Betty
Smith, Elinor Goulding
Smith, Frank
Smith, Logan Pearsall
Smith, Preserved
Smith, Sydney
Smith, W.B.
Smith, William Cooper
Smoller, Jordan W.
Smollett, Tobias
Snow, Dan
Sobol, Thomas
Sockman, Ralph M.
Socrates
Soichiro, Honda
Solis, Alicia
Solon
Sophocles
Southby, Robert
Southey, Robert
Spady, William G.
Spencer, Herbert
Spock, Benjamin
St. Ambrose
St. Augustine
St. John, George
St. Paul
St. Thomas Aquinas
Stack, Jack

Stafford, William
Stalin, Joseph
Standing, E. M.
Steadman, Edward C.
Steele, Sir Richard
Stein, Gertrude
Steinbeck, John
Steiner, Rudolf
Stellar, W. C.
Stendhal
Stephen, Leslie
Sterne, Laurence
Stevenson, Adlai E.
Stevenson, Robert Louis
Stockdale, James B.
Steoessinger, John G.
Stone, Joseph
Stone, W. Clement
Stoppard, Tom
Stovall, Jim
Stravinsky, Igor
Streightiff, Walt
Strujar, Margaret
Style, Lylee
Sturgeon, Nicola
Sufi Saint Kubir
Sugarman, Sidney
Sullivan, Anne
Sweetland, Ben
Swift, Jonathan
Swindoll, Charles
Swope, Herbert Bayard
Sydney Mith of Macaulay
Syrus, Publilius
Szasz, Thomas
Szent-Györgyi

T
Tabor, Mary B.W.
Tacitus
Tagore, Rabindranath
Taine, Hippolyte Adolphe
Talbert, Bob
Tauscher, Stacia
Taylor, Elizabeth
Taylor, Harold
Tempah, Tinie
Temple, William
Templeton, John
Tennyson, Alfred Lord
Terence
Theisman, Joe
Thomas, Dylan
Thomas, Lewis
Thomas, Lowell
Thompson, Dorothy
Thomson, James
Thoreau, Henry David
Thucydies
Thurber, James
Ting-Fang, Wu
Tiong, Ho Boon
Toffler, Alvin
Tolkien, J. R. R.
Tolstoy, Leo
Tomlin, Lily
Toomer, Jean
Toynbee, Arnold J.
Tracy, Brian
Traherne, Thomas
Traub, James
Treisman, Uri
Trench, R.C.

Those Quoted

Trevelyan, G.M.
Trilling, Lionel
Trollope, Anthony
Trotter, Charlie
Troy, Frosty
Truman, Harry S.
Trump, Donald
Trump, J. Lloyd
Tse-Tung, Mao
Tsvetaeva, Marina
Tuchman, Barbara
Tupper, Martin
Tutu, Desmond
Twain, Mark
Tyger, Frank
Tzu, Lao
Tzu, Sun

U

Upanishads
Updike, John
Usiskin, Zalman
Ustinov, Peter
Valvano, Jim

V

van Beethoven, Ludwig
Van Buren, Abigail "Dear Abby"
Van Doren, Mark
Van Dyke, Henry
van Gogh, Vincent
Vanderbilt, Cornelius
Vaughan, Bill
Vauvenargues, Marquis de

Venkatachalm, V.
Verdi, R.
Vespasianus, Titus
Victor, Jodie
Vidal, Gore
Viguers, Ruth Hill
Viorst, Judith
Virgil
Vivekananda, Swami
Volkart, Edmund H.
Voltaire
Von Goethe, Johann Wolfgang
von Hardenberg, Friedrich
Vonnegut, Kurt

W

Wagner, Victoria
Waitley, Denis
Walker, Lou Ann
Wallace, Lew
Walters, Barbara
Walton, Izaak
Walton, Sam
Ward, William Arthur
Warhol, Andy
Warner, Charles Dudley
Warren, Earl
Warren, John
Warren, Rick
Washburn, Lemuel K.
Washington, Booker T.
Washington, George
Watson, Sr., Thomas
Waugh, Evelyn
Waxman, Isabel

Wayne, John
Weaver, Earl
Weber, Max
Webster, Daniel
Weierstrass, Karl
Weil, Simone
Wells, H. G.
Welles, Orson
Welty, Eudora
Welsh, Joan
Wendell Holmes, Oliver
Wenn, Jonathan
Wesley, John
West, Jessamyn
West, Nathaniel
West, Walt
Wharton, Edith
Whipple, Edwin Perry
Whistler, James McNeil
White, E.B.
White, T.H.
White, W.J.
Whitehead, Alfred North
Whitman, Walt
Whitmore, Frank
Whyte, Lancelot Law
Wiesel, Elie
Wiggan, A. E.
Wilbur, Ray L.
Wilcox, Colleen
Wilde, Larry
Wilde, Oscar
Wilde, Stuart
Wilkens, Lenny
Willard, Frances
Wilson, Eugene S.

401

Those Quoted

Wilson, Sloan
Wilson, Tom
Wilson, Woodrow
Winchell, Walter
Winder, Barbara W.
Winfrey, Oprah
Winston, Alan
   Scott
Witherspoon, Reese
Wittgenstein, Ludwig
Wolfe, Thomas
Wollstonecraft, Mary
Wonder, Stevie

Wong, Harry
Wood, David
Wood, Sydney
Wooden, John
Woolf, Virginia
Wordsworth, William
Wright, Frank Lloyd
Wright, Steven
Wylie, Philip

Y
Yates, Richard
Yeatman, R. J.

Yeats, W. B.
Yeats-Brown,
   Francis
Yohe, Tom
Young, Brigham
Young, Neil
Yutang, Lin

Z
Zappa, Frank
Zeidner, M. A.
Ziglar, Zig
Zola, Emile